The Book of
SENIOR
MOMENTS

The Book of
SENIOR
MOMENTS

Shelley Klein

Michael O'Mara Books Limited

This paperback edition first published in 2020
First published in Great Britain in 2006 by
Michael O'Mara Books Limited
9 Lion Yard
Tremadoc Road
London SW4 7NQ

A CIP catalogue record for this book is available from the British Library.

Papers used by Michael O'Mara Books Limited are natural, recyclable
products made from wood grown in sustainable forests. The
manufacturing processes conform to the environmental regulations of the
country of origin.

ISBN: 978-1-78929-226-8 in paperback print format
ISBN: 978-1-84317-433-2 in ebook format

3 4 5 6 7 8 9 10

Designed and typeset by Design 23

Printed and bound by CPI Group (UK) Ltd, Croydon, CR0 4YY

CONTENTS

'I think the life cycle is all backwards. You should die first, get it out of the way. Then you live in an old-age home. You get kicked out when you're too young, you get a gold watch, you go to work. You work forty years until you're young enough to enjoy your retirement. You do drugs, alcohol, you party, you get ready for high school. You go to grade school, you become a kid, you play, you have no responsibilities, you become a little baby, you go back into the womb, you spend your last nine months floating . . . and you finish off as an orgasm.'

GEORGE CARLIN, COMEDIAN

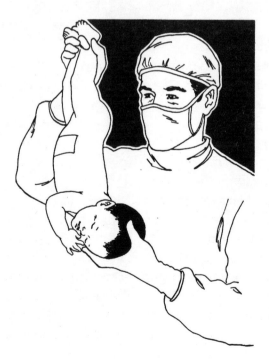

INTRODUCTION

There is only one period of our lives during which we consciously desire to be older than we actually are, and that is childhood. When we are less than fifteen years old, we are so excited about 'growing up' we tend to think in fractions, leading us to tell people proudly that we are ten-and-a-half or nine-and-three-quarters. Sadly, however, this lust for maturity doesn't last long and by the time we hit our mid-twenties and realize that our youth is well and truly behind us, we'd do anything to slow down time's passage.

Although we can be sure that age will eventually catch up with each and every one of us, what is less certain is precisely how early the first signs of ageing will occur. After all, if you're in your thirties when your best friend's name mysteriously begins to elude you, what does that say about you? Even at this early age, you may well be experiencing your first senior moment, after which life will never quite be the same! Senior moments are perhaps best described as the sort of mental blips that waylay us at the most inconvenient times; sometimes leading to confusion and calamity, they can be infuriating and entertaining in equal measure. One thing you can be sure of – as this book testifies – is that you are certainly not alone.

Senior moments can strike even the best of us at an early age and the usual reaction to this anomaly is one of utter incredulity– 'I didn't just do or say that, did I?' No self-respecting person in their thirties or forties wants to be told that their brains, let alone their bodies, are already beginning to decline and fail. However cruel it may seem, if the name of those oval-shaped objects you keep in the fridge which you can fry, boil or scramble for breakfast, is proving more difficult to conjure up than world peace, it may

9

be time to face the music and embrace this new, brain-addled chapter of your life.

Overnight – or so it appears – you start forgetting your own phone number. Then you mix your phone number up with your PIN number, followed swiftly by attempting to use your PIN number to access your credit card account. The day before yesterday you managed to mistake next door's house for your own and tried to unlock the front door, only to realize that instead of picking up the house keys on the way out you accidentally grabbed the keys to the garden shed. Okay, so you are unlikely to win the award for most switched-on person of the year, but don't go booking yourself in to a lunatic asylum (at least not yet), for all of the above are yet more examples of senior moments. Enjoy them, relish them, laugh at them, bask in them, but most of all – get used to having them, because from the moment they first rear their mischievous little heads, they will continue to plague you for the rest of your life.

From the musings of Cicero to the irony of Oscar Wilde; from the sheer frustration of J. B. Priestley to the witty verse of Ogden Nash; writers throughout the ages have contributed greatly and with evident relish to this universal subject. The creator of the curmudgeonly Rumpole of the Bailey, the inimitable John Mortimer, has written a beautiful piece in his book *The Summer of a Dormouse* about the difficulty of putting on one's socks once you reach a certain age, and the inability of those younger than yourself to consider this will ever happen to them. It is, he says both a 'humiliating and comical' experience. But, if these senior moments leave you feeling a little down or depressed, then you could do worse than consider Voltaire's advice and go on living simply in order 'to enrage' everyone around you, or take comfort from Doris Lessing's observation that having reached the age where she is 'invisible', she has gained tremendous freedom to do and act as she likes! Another way in which you could combat the senior moment blues, is – like several of the entries in this volume illustrate – to write to *The Times*. Allan H. Briggs did just this regarding a restaurant advertising 'special reductions for old-age pensioners'. The result, however, wasn't quite as anticipated.

Finally, but by no means least importantly, don't miss out on the lifestyle sections of this book which offer some very simple ways in which you might help improve your memory, giving tips on diet and exercise, as well as recreational activities such as bridge and crossword puzzles which can play a vital role in keeping your mind as active as possible. One cannot put enough emphasis on eating healthily and all foods detailed in this volume (i.e. oily fish, fresh fruit, vegetables, nuts, lean meat and pulses) have been shown to be beneficial, particularly when it comes to improving brain function, as has exercise and keeping active.

But the most important thing of all to remember is that when a senior moment does strike, do not feel foolish, annoyed or embarrassed, because it's certain that everyone, from the lowliest brain to the world's greatest thinkers, has suffered the same.

EARLY SIGNS

Often, although we suspect we've begun experiencing senior moments, rather than recognizing the warning signs and acknowledging the facts, we bury our heads in the sand or, worse still, turn tail and run. Of course, these avoidance tactics are about as useful as a sledgehammer to the head. Here are some ways to detect whether you too are in the grip of this dreaded phenomenon:

You start calling your best friend of twenty-five years 'Thingy'.

You discover that your car has mysteriously parked itself on the other side of the road.

You could paint a picture of it, write a thesis about it, demonstrate how to use it to Olympic standard . . . but you can't for the life of you remember its name.

When you stand at the bottom of the stairs, you can't recall whether you were just about to go up to fetch something or whether you've just come down to fetch something.

You try to straighten out the wrinkles in your socks – and discover you aren't wearing any.

You put all the photos you own into a large album, but, try as you might, you can't remember who any of the people are in the photographs.

You've started forgetting simple words such as . . . umm, uhhh, ahh . . .

Gravity is no longer a term confined to science or geography textbooks, but increasingly refers to your body.

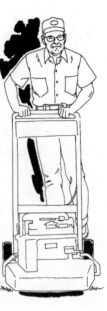

Lawn care has become the highlight of your life.

You sink your teeth into a steak . . . and leave them there.

Your partner says, 'Let's go upstairs and make love,' and you reply, 'Pick one, I can't do both.'

You know exactly how to play bridge, canasta and Mah Jong – worse still, you look forward to playing them every weekend with your friends.

You're very good at opening a childproof cap . . . with a hammer.

The list of things you hate begins to outnumber the list of things you like.

You experience permanent jet lag, yet the last time you stepped on a plane was five years ago.

At the breakfast table you hear 'snap, crackle, pop' and you're not even eating cereal.

You start prefixing every word with 'little' – e.g. 'I'll just have a little lie-down', 'I'll just fix myself a little drink', etc. . . .

You begin every sentence with 'Nowadays'.

You bend down to pick something up off the floor, then begin wondering what else you could do while you're down there.

You tend to go to restaurants that don't play music – this way you can enjoy hearing what everyone is saying.

You ring someone up but the moment they answer the phone you forget a) who you are calling, b) why you are calling, and c) why you are still living at all.

When you're on holiday your energy runs out before your money.

You begin laying the table for breakfast at six o'clock the previous evening.

You start listening with slightly more concern to any news items containing the word 'pension'.

When you arrive at a party you immediately start planning the time of your departure.

You begin scheduling long car journeys and shopping trips around the number of known public conveniences on your trip.

You start answering your phone . . . when it rings on television.

You've thrown out your back trying to open a can of pilchards.

You start going through red traffic lights, but stopping at green ones.

You are paying more and more attention to the government's advice on how to keep warm during the winter.

You're on first-name terms with your pharmacist.

You know the difference between a gastroenterologist, a urologist and an osteopath.

You accidentally open your outgoing post . . . on a regular basis.

Rather than opting for G-strings or bikini-style underwear, you are sporting the sort of pants that could double as a parachute.

You are the last to admit that your 'get up and go' has got up and left.

Your friends compliment you on the new alligator shoes you're wearing, while you're barefoot.

A FEW WORDS OF WISDOM FROM J. B. PRIESTLEY

'Tendency to delay putting on trousers because one foot is standing on braces. Odd recent behaviour of pipes scattering sparks and hot ashes on carpets and lapels of coats. Going upstairs for something and forgetting on the way what on earth it was. Remembering in detail the face, voice, name, habits, of a man in 1909, but no clues to the man who called last week and is coming again this afternoon. Inability to wade through important leading articles. Growing horror of stag parties, whether pompous or drunken, and sharp preference for feminine company, though not in large groups. Distinct signs of nausea produced by the sight and sound of shaggy young men playing electric guitars and belting out one idiotic phrase over and over again.'
– *OUTCRIES AND ASIDES*, 1974

MORE EARLY SIGNS

'Old age is like everything else. To make a success of it, you've got to start young.' – FRED ASTAIRE, DANCER, SINGER AND ACTOR

'You know you're getting old when high-court judges start looking young to you.' – RONNIE GOLDEN, STAND-UP COMEDIAN

'To me old age is fifteen years older than I am.' – BERNARD M. BARUCH, FINANCIER AND STATESMAN

'There are three signs of old age: loss of memory . . . I forget the other two.' – RED SKELTON, ACTOR

'You know you are getting older if you
have more fingers than real teeth.'
– Rodney Dangerfield, comedian

'Age considers; youth ventures.'
– Rabindranath Tagore, poet and philosopher

'Age is a matter of feeling, not of years.'
– George William Curtis, writer

'You know you're getting old when all the names in your black book
have MD after them.' – Harrison Ford, actor

'That phrase they use, "in living memory" – as in, "the worst
floods in living memory" or "the coldest winter in living memory"
– just how far back does it stretch? Because at my age, my "living
memory" goes back to a week last Tuesday.' – Alan Coren,
journalist and writer

'One of the signs of old age is that you have to carry your senses
around in your handbag – glasses, hearing aid, dentures.'
– Kurt Strauss

'You remind me of a poem I can't remember, and a song that may
never have existed, and a place I'm not sure I've ever been to.'
– Grampa Simpson, *The Simpsons*

'Remembering something at first try is now as good as an orgasm
as far as I'm concerned.' – Gloria Steinem, feminist and journalist

'Spare a thought for my friend Eliza Hamilton, who was wrongly diagnosed as mentally unstable when all she was, was a bit giddy.'
– MRS MERTON, *THE MRS MERTON SHOW*

'The face is familiar, but I can't remember my name.'
– ROBERT BENCHLEY, COMEDIAN

'An uncle of mine, a retired headmaster, said that the first time he felt old was when he was in a queue at his local post office to collect his pension and found himself behind a former pupil who was there for the same purpose.' – PAUL KELVIN-SMITH

'Signs you're getting on a bit: your back hurts; you eat food past its sell-by date; your carpet is patterned; you go supermarket shopping in the evening to pick up marked-down bargains; you can spell; you hang your clothes on padded coat hangers; you save the hearing-aid flyer that falls out of the colour supplement; you try to get electrical gadgets repaired when they go wrong; you save the free little packets of sugar from cafés; you have worn a knitted swimsuit; when you watch black-and-white films you spend the whole time pointing at the screen going, "He's dead . . . She's dead . . . "; your car stereo is tuned to Radio 2.' – COLIN SLATER, RADIO DJ

'My memory's starting to go. The only thing I still retain is water.'
– ALEX COLE, BASEBALL PLAYER

'You know you're getting old when you go on holiday and always pack a sweater.' – DENIS NORDEN, COMEDIAN AND TV PRESENTER

'As you get older, you've probably noticed that you tend to forget things. You'll be talking at a party, and you'll know that you know this person, but no matter how hard you try, you can't remember his or her name. This can be very embarrassing, especially if he or she turns out to be your spouse.' – DAVE BARRY, WRITER AND COMEDIAN

'You know you're getting old when your wife believes your excuses for getting home late.' – BASIL RANSOME-DAVIES

'I've started wearing cardigans and saying things like "Whoopsadaisy", and when I take a first sip of tea, "Ooh, that hits the spot!"' – GARY, *MEN BEHAVING BADLY*

'I knew I was getting old when the Pope started looking young.' – BILLY WILDER, SCREENWRITER AND PRODUCER

'I've started wearing cardigans and saying things like 'You know you're getting old when you're dashing through Marks & Spencer, spot a pair of Dr Scholl's sandals, stop, and think, "Hmm, they look comfy."' – VICTORIA WOOD, COMEDIAN

'Whenever a man's friends begin to compliment him about looking young, he may be sure that they think he is growing old.' – WASHINGTON IRVING, WRITER

'I contemplated buying a new cream that claimed to stop the seven signs of ageing and wondered what they might be. Talking about the weather? Wearing slippers? Memory loss? Compulsive need to queue up at the post office? Memory loss? Inability to comprehend the lyrics of pop songs?' – MARIA MCERLANE, NEWSPAPER COLUMNIST

'You know you're getting old when you're interested in going home before you get to where you're going.' – ALAN MAINWARING

'You know you're getting old when you and your partner wear matching sweaters.' – MARK SCHOFIELD

'You know you're getting old when you start to like your mum and dad again. "Yes, Mum, I'd love to come caravanning to Tenby with you. No, I'll bring a packed lunch. I'm not paying café prices."' – JEFF GREEN, COMEDIAN

THE BEST OF FRIENDS?

Two well-bred Englishwomen of a certain age, friends for many years, met once a week in Oxford in order to go shopping; that done, they would then always reward themselves with tea at Fuller's.

On one occasion, they had settled at their table and ordered tea and slices of the famous walnut cake, when a look of absolute horror passed across the face of one of the ladies. Clearly deeply troubled, she turned to her companion and said:

'My dear, the most dreadful thing has happened. We have been friends for so many years, we see each other regularly and speak often, but suddenly and unaccountably, I have forgotten your name. I am sure that it will come to me in a moment, but could you possibly just tell me what it is? I really am most dreadfully sorry . . . '

Her friend stared at her in silence, frowning and obviously thinking very hard. The pause lengthened, as she gave all her attention to what her companion had just said. Finally, after the wait had lengthened to some minutes, she replied: 'When do you need to know by?'

HOW TIME FLIES

At an old soldiers' club, an old field marshal says to an equally old major general, 'Um, tell me, Charles, when did you last have sex with a woman?'

Charles scratches his head, ponders for a while and eventually answers: 'About 1946, I think, William. What about you, old chap?'

William sighs and replies, 'That would be, um, 1948, I think.'

Charles shakes his head slowly and says, 'A long time ago, old boy, a long time ago.'

'Oh, I don't know,' says William, 'It's only just gone half past nine now, you know.'

FAMILY REUNION

An elderly man in Australia calls his son in London and says, 'I hate to ruin your day, but I have to let you know that your mother and I have decided to separate – forty years of misery is enough for anybody.'

'Dad, I can't believe it!' his son exclaims.

'We can't stand the sight of each other, any longer,' the old man says. 'We're sick of each other, and I'm fed up of talking about it, so you call your sister in New York and tell her.' He hangs up the phone. Out of his mind with worry, the son calls his sister, who explodes down the phone.

'They simply cannot get a divorce,' she shouts. 'Leave it to me.' She calls her father immediately and screams at the old man, 'You are not divorcing Mum! Please don't do a single thing until I get there. I'll call my brother now and we'll both be there tomorrow morning. Until then, don't do a thing, promise me?' and she hangs up. The old man puts down the receiver and turns to his wife. 'Okay,' he says, 'They're coming for Christmas and they're paying their own air fares.'

IT'S A NUMBERS THING

'I can lie convincingly about my age because at my age I can't always remember what it is.' – VIOLET CONTI

'Now I must turn my questing violet eyes to 1969. My seventieth year! There is really no comment to make about that except perhaps, "Well, well", "Fancy", or "Oh fuck".' – NOEL COWARD, *THE NOEL COWARD DIARIES*

'I have no patience with the people who grow old at sixty just because they are entitled to a bus pass. Sixty should be the time to start something new, not put your feet up.' – MARY WESLEY, WRITER

'We're obsessed with age. Numbers are always and pointlessly attached to every name that's published in a newspaper: "Joe Creamer, forty-three, and his daughter, Tiffany-Ann, nine, were merrily chasing a bunny, two,when Tiffany-Ann tripped on the root of a tree, 106."' – JOAN RIVERS, COMEDIAN

'Your forties, you grow a little pot belly, you grow another chin. The music starts to get too loud and one of your old girlfriends from high school becomes a grandmother. Your fifties, you have a minor surgery. You'll call it a procedure, but it's a surgery. Your sixties, you have a major surgery, the music is still loud but it doesn't matter because you can't hear it anyway. Seventies, you and the wife retire to Fort Lauderdale, you start eating dinner at two, lunch around ten, breakfast the night before. And you spend most of your time wandering around malls, looking for the ultimate in soft yoghurt and muttering, "How come the kids don't call?" By your eighties, you've had a major stroke, and you end up babbling to some Jamaican nurse who your wife can't stand, but who you call "mamma". Any questions?' – MITCH ROBBINS, *CITY SLICKERS*

'I'm not interested in age. People who tell me their age are silly. You're as old as you feel.' – ELIZABETH ARDEN, BUSINESSWOMAN

'The hardest years in life are those between ten and seventy.' – HELEN HAYES, ACTRESS

'My sister, Jackie, is younger than me. We don't know quite by how much.' – JOAN COLLINS, ACTRESS AND WRITER

'In a dream you are never eighty.' – ANNE SEXTON, POET AND WRITER

'Sex at the age of eighty-four is a wonderful experience. Especially the one in the winter.' – MILTON BERLE, COMEDIAN

'At the end of this year I shall be sixty-three – if alive – and about the same if dead.' – MARK TWAIN, WRITER

'I got nervous when I was asked to play God. We're both around the same age, but we grew up in different neighbourhoods.' – GEORGE BURNS, ACTOR AND WRITER

'The years between fifty and seventy are the hardest. You are always being asked to do things, and you are not yet decrepit enough to turn them down.' – T. S. ELIOT, POET

'At twenty we worry about what others think of us; at forty we don't care about what others think of us; at sixty we discover they haven't been thinking about us at all.' – ANON

'Two weeks ago we celebrated my uncle's 103rd birthday. 103 – isn't that something? Unfortunately he wasn't present. How could he be? He died when he was twenty-nine.' – VICTOR BORGE, COMEDIAN

'People ask me what I'd most appreciate getting for my eighty-seventh birthday. I tell them, a paternity suit.' – GEORGE BURNS, ACTOR AND WRITER

'I'm eighty, but in my own mind, my age veers. When I'm performing on stage, I'm forty; when I'm shopping in Waitrose, I'm 120.' – HUMPHREY LYTTELTON, JAZZ MUSICIAN

'I refuse to admit that I am more than fifty-two, even if that does make my sons illegitimate.' – NANCY ASTOR, SOCIALITE AND POLITICIAN

'I had a huge party for my seventieth birthday with 800 guests. With so many familiar faces there it was like driving through the rear-view mirror.' – PETER USTINOV, WRITER AND ACTOR

BACKSEAT DRIVER

An elderly lady dials the police to report that her car has been broken into. She is hysterical as she explains her situation. 'The monsters have stolen the stereo, the steering wheel, the brake pedal and even the accelerator!' she cries. The operator asks her to remain calm and informs her that a police officer is on his way. A few minutes later, the officer radios in his report. 'Disregard,' he says. 'She got in the backseat by mistake.'

POOTLE'S STORY

Have you ever wondered why dogs never get tired of fetching sticks, or why, even if you've only left the house for five minutes, your four-legged friend always greets you as if you've been away for five years? The answer is quite simple – he's suffering from senior momentitis. Indeed, your beloved Fido could probably write a whole book on the subject, if he could write that is, and if he could remember where he buried the pen. Cats, on the other hand, are far superior creatures . . . or are they?

Enter the tale of Pootle, a beautiful marmalade feline, nearing his dotage. Over a period of a few weeks Pootle increasingly had been plagued by the unwanted attentions of a feral cat who had modelled himself on A Nightmare on Elm Street villain Freddy Krueger. Every time Pootle ventured through his cat flap there ensued a brawl of considerable ferocity. Claws were drawn, teeth bared and fur was sent flying, as the neighbours were subjected to a caterwauling worthy of The X Factor. Mrs Smith, Pootle's owner, later remarked that on the sole occasion she caught a glimpse of 'Freddy', she understood why Pootle so anxiously crossed his legs and hovered nervously around the door whenever he was in town. The Smiths convened; it was decided that action was required, and so Mrs Smith dutifully trotted to the RSPCA to pick up a cat trap.

Setting the trap up was easy enough. Mrs Smith placed some lovely tinned tuna at one end, carefully balanced the door on its prop and set the whole contraption up in the garden. Nor did she have to wait long for the results. On hearing the metal door slam shut, she rushed eagerly into the garden – only to find Pootle sitting inside, disgruntled and glowering. Reasoning that any normal cat, once released, would not go near the contraption again, Mrs Smith undid the latch and set Pootle free. But Pootle was no ordinary cat. On the first day alone of owning the trap, Mrs Smith 'caught' Pootle a total of fourteen times. A number of the neighbours' cats were also caught. In fact, the only cat that wasn't captured that day was Freddy Krueger.

Nor were the second day's attempts any more fruitful, for it seemed that Pootle simply could not recall having been caught in the trap beyond a couple of minutes. Each time his owner came to the rescue, there he sat in the cage, a quizzical look etched upon his features as if to say: 'I think I've been here before.'

Proof at last that animals fall foul to the dreaded senior momentitis too.

IT'S ALL DOWNHILL

'Growing old is like being increasingly penalized for a crime you haven't committed.' – ANTHONY POWELL, WRITER

'Years ago we discovered the exact point, the dead centre of middle age. It occurs when you are too young to take up golf and too old to rush to the goal.' – FRANKLIN PIERCE ADAMS, JOURNALIST

'Middle age is when your age starts to show around your middle.'
– BOB HOPE, ENTERTAINER

'I am at that age. Too young for the bowling green, too old for Ecstasy.' – RAB C. NESBITT

'In the middle of the nineteenth century, an Englishman named Robert Browning wrote: "Grow old along with me, the best is yet to be." Clearly this man was a minor poet.' – JOAN RIVERS, COMEDIAN

'One problem with growing older is that it gets increasingly tougher to find a famous historical figure who didn't amount to much when he was your age.' – BILL VAUGHAN, JOURNALIST

'Many people die at twenty-five and aren't buried until they're seventy-five.' – MAX FRISCH, ARCHITECT AND PLAYWRIGHT

'I'm forty-three, and for the first time this year I have felt older. I'm slowly becoming more decrepit. I think you just move to the country and wear an old fleece.' – JENNIFER SAUNDERS, COMEDIAN

'Forty is the old age of youth; fifty the youth of old age.'
– VICTOR HUGO, WRITER

'In youth the days are short and the years are long; in old age the years are short and the days long.' – NIKITA IVANOVICH PANIN, POLITICIAN

'There is absolutely nothing to be said in favour of growing old. There ought to be legislation against it.' – SIR PATRICK MOORE, ASTRONOMER AND TV PRESENTER

'I don't believe that one grows older. I think that what happens early on in life is that at a certain age one stands still and stagnates.' – T.S. ELIOT, POET

ANCIENT WORDS OF WISDOM

'My dear Laelius and Scipio, we must stand up against old age and make up for its drawbacks by taking pains. We must fight it as we should an illness. We must look after our health, use moderate exercise, take just enough food and drink to recover, but not to overload, our strength. Nor is it the body alone that must be supported, but the intellect and soul much more. For they are like lamps, unless you feed them with oil, they too go out from old age . . . The fact is that old age is respectable just as long as it asserts itself, maintains its proper rights, and is not enslaved to anyone. For as I admire a young man who has something of the old man in him, so do I an old one who has something of a young man. The man who aims at this may possibly become old in body – in mind he never will.' – CICERO, ON OLD AGE

DEAR SIR

The letters page of The Times has long been a vehicle for members of the British public to, among other things, vent their spleen, point out humorous observations, or take umbrage with the world. Here are a few examples of all three:

'Sir, I recently dined at a pretentious local hotel. When presented with an exorbitant bill for an indifferent meal, I drew the waiter's attention to a prominent notice which offered "Special reductions for old-age pensioners".

"That, sir," he explained disdainfully, "relates not to our charges, but to the size of the portions."

We have been warned.'

Yours etc.,

Allan H. Briggs, Lincoln

'Sir, a British Gas salesman, replacing a defective heating boiler, told me: "The makers will tell you this boiler will give twenty-five years' service." He looked up at me, hesitated, and continued: "But of course to you that would not be a selling point."'

Kenneth J. Bruce, Kings Lynn

'Sir, as a child I regarded elderly people as upholders of the standards of common courtesy and behaviour towards others. Now in our thirties, my wife and I increasingly observe that senior citizens are displaying poor manners. They often fail to acknowledge a door held open or the offer of a seat on a train; we are regularly jostled in queues by "oldies" who appear unwilling to wait their turn. Have I become intolerant or is the present generation of senior citizens less polite?'

Yours faithfully,

Christopher Nelms, Hampshire

KEEP DEATH OFF THE ROADS

A sixty-five-year-old man had just driven on to the motorway when his car phone rang. Answering it, he found his wife on the other end of the line. 'Bert,' she said urgently, 'Be careful. I've just heard on the news that there's a car driving the wrong way up the motorway.'

'Hell,' he replied. 'It's not just one – there are hundreds of them!'

For reasons known only to the gods, senior moments frequently strike while we're either driving our cars or trying to locate them after we've parked. Indeed, it might be observed from the following quotations that growing old and successfully handling a motor vehicle are seemingly incompatible . . .

'What is the age people reach when they decide, when they back out of the driveway, they're not looking any more? You know how they do that? They just go, "Well, I'm old, and I'm backing out. I survived, let's see if you can."' – JERRY SEINFELD, ACTOR AND COMEDIAN

'They say the first thing to go when you're old is your legs or your eyesight. It isn't true. The first thing to go is parallel parking.' – KURT VONNEGUT, WRITER

'Sir, would you let Helen Mound know that the over-sixties don't all drive Rovers and wear flat caps ('Motoring', January 5)? In fact, I drive a Subaru Impreza Turbo.' – JOHN MILTON, STANSTEAD, ABBOTS, HERTS *THE DAILY TELEGRAPH*

'Mr Merton is getting on in years but he's still driving. I do worry as sometimes he forgets to indicate but he always says, "I've lived in the same road for forty years and I think people know where I'm going by now."' – MRS MERTON, *THE MRS MERTON SHOW*

'One of the delights of being a senior citizen is it's easy to annoy young people. Step 1) Get in the car. Step 2) Turn the indicator on. Step 3) Leave it on for fifty miles.' – DAVID LETTERMAN, TALK-SHOW HOST

'In my day, no one had cars. If you wanted to get run over, you'd catch a bus to the main road . . . And we didn't do all this keep-fit. We got our exercise lowering coffins out of upstairs windows.' – VICTORIA WOOD, *OLD BAG*

PETER'S STORY

A man nearing his fortieth birthday was out driving, chatting to his wife about his impending seniordom. Peter was regaling Rowenna with stories about just how young he felt. He wasn't suffering from any aches and pains, he could still touch his toes, play tennis, stay up late drinking, yet get up the next morning fresh as a daisy.

Now only the week before, Rowenna had visited her doctor complaining of a persistent pain in her left leg. The doctor had very kindly asked when she was born, after which he surmised her complaint was probably just old age catching up with her. He also ran some tests to make sure it wasn't anything more sinister, but when she had told Peter about the visit, he had hooted with laughter and kept teasing her about her oncoming senility.

Soon Peter set about comparing himself to his wife. His body was a work of art, his mind a steel trap, there was nothing he couldn't overcome either physically or mentally. If his wife only stopped seeing herself as old, he suggested, and instead showed the same enthusiasm and lust for life that he did, then maybe she would start to feel and look as energetic and fit as he himself did.

Parking outside an antiques shop, they had both climbed out of the car, when suddenly it began to move. The silly old man had not only forgotten to put the handbrake on, but also failed to move out of the car's way in time. The vehicle lurched forward, knocking Peter sideways and causing him to fall over and break his ankle. As if this wasn't enough, a gaggle of schoolkids wandered past at this precise moment and assembled to watch as Peter hobbled to his feet.

'Alright, grandad?' they screamed.

Face burning red, Peter climbed back into the car with his wife's help and sat, red-faced and silent, all the way to A&E.

GRUMPY OLD PEOPLE

Senior moments often go hand in hand with grumpy thoughts. Indeed, railing against the world is a sure sign that you are heading towards your dotage. Here are a few prime examples:

'Pensioners are by far the worst drivers. They are spiteful, dithering, old and in the way. They should have their licences taken away.' – JEREMY CLARKSON, MOTORING JOURNALIST AND TV PRESENTER

'Call those pants? I can remember when pants were pants. You wore them for twenty years, then you cut them down for pan scrubs.'– VICTORIA WOOD, OLD BAG

'At a certain age, you begin to snort at fashion, you stop going to the cinema and you watch the black-and-white classic on aeroplanes. You slouch into a curmudgeonly comfort culture of the old and familiar, and become a "call that" person. "Call that music/fashion/ poetry/a chair?"' – A. A. GILL, NEWSPAPER COLUMNIST AND WRITER

'The only time I've ever been rendered speechless with fury was when some daft television presenter opened a programme aimed at senior travellers by asking what sort of holidays were "suitable" for them.' – ELISABETH DE STROUMILLO, WRITER

'In my day, a juvenile delinquent was a kid who owed tuppence on an overdue library book.' – MAX BYGRAVES, SINGER AND SONGWRITER

'In my day, we never got woken up by a Teasmade. We were knocked up every morning by a man with a six-foot pole. And we weren't having hysterectomies every two minutes either, like the girls these days. If something went wrong down below, you kept your gob shut and turned up the wireless.' – VICTORIA WOOD, *OLD BAG*

'In my day, men wore driving gloves, women stayed married, and curry had raisins in it.' – SWISS TONY, *THE FAST SHOW*

'If you are sufficiently irascible, God might just decide to wait.' – GODFREY JUST

'When you are about thirty-five years old, something terrible always happens to music.' – STEVE RACE, BROADCASTER, MUSICIAN AND AUTHOR

PARKING IS SUCH SWEET SORROW

A gentleman in his mid-forties found himself increasingly exasperated over his wife's extensive collection of parking tickets. While other people collected sensible items such as old dolls' heads, empty bottles and egg cups in the shape of Margaret Thatcher, this particular lady was the proud owner of a collection of penalties dating as far back as 1980, obtained from such exotic climes as Los Angeles, Melbourne, Belgrade and a tiny French village in the Pyrenees called Cauterets; a ticket which was especially dear to its owner, on the basis of its having been presented to her by the mayor.

With such a fine track record, perhaps she shouldn't have been so aggravated when, upon announcing to her husband that she was 'off into town' for a spot of shopping, her husband jumped up from what he was doing and rushed into his study and emerged clutching a bag of one-pound coins.

'For the parking meters,' he said, smiling sweetly.

'And who says I'm going to use one?' she snapped back. 'I might decide to park on the outside of town and walk in.'

'Well, why don't you take them . . . just in case,' he murmured soothingly.

'Just in case of what? I'm not a total imbecile,' she fired back, before departing with the bag of coins begrudgingly held in one hand and her car keys in the other.

On reaching town, she parked the car and soon found herself in that wonderful comfort zone of clothes shopping, followed by an espresso, followed by more clothes shopping, followed by a spot of light lunch. By the time she arrived home, she had purchased two beautiful skirts, a digital wonder watch that could tell the temperature in four time zones and speak five different languages, some new jeans and a pair of shorts for her husband. Entering the house, she had a sinking feeling that the shopping expedition hadn't gone entirely to plan.

'Good day?', her husband enquired innocently, as she thoughtfully poured herself a large gin and tonic.

'Fantastic,' she said brightly, turning towards him. 'You're going to love the shorts I bought you!'

'No, um, parking tickets?' he asked.

'No,' she said, quietly. 'No parking tickets.' He grinned and kissed his wife affectionately.

'That's brilliant,' he said. 'So we should always keep a bag of coins in the car, eh?'

'Yup,' she nodded, then glanced down at her digital wonder watch, hoping that it might somehow provide her with a helpful solution, but it only managed to tell her the time in Afghanistan.

'Good thinking. Now why don't you go upstairs and try on the shorts?'

Never one to shirk his duties, her husband readily jumped up from the sofa and bounded upstairs to the bedroom. Just enough time for his wife to shout out that she had to pop out for a moment and hastily beat a retreat via the bus, back into town to pick up the car. Not only had she forgotten to put money in the meter, but she had spent the bag of coins on a taxi ride home, exhausted after a long and arduous day of retail therapy . . .

LOVE POTIONS

A man aged eighty-five and his eighty-year-old fiancée are over the moon about their decision to get married. One afternoon, they are taking a walk in order to discuss their impending nuptials when they pass a chemist and Albert suggests that they go in. Entering the shop, he approaches the gentleman behind the counter and asks whether he is the owner. The pharmacist nods politely.

'Do you sell heart medication?' asks Albert cheerfully.

'Of course we do, sir,' replies the pharmacist and he reaches behind the counter and produces the requested item.

'How about medicine for high blood pressure?'

The pharmacist again nods and produces another package from behind the counter.

'Medicine for arthritis?'

'Yes, sir.'

'What about sleeping pills?'

'Yes, of course.'

'Vitamins?'

'Yes, a number of different types.'

'Oh, and do you stock Viagra?'

'Certainly.'

'That's great! We'd like to register here for our wedding gifts.'

WISE COUNSEL?

'[The late barrister] Patrick Pakenham became something of a legal legend . . . As defence counsel in a complicated fraud case, he was due to address the court during the afternoon session, and had partaken of a particularly well-oiled lunch. "Members of the jury, it is my duty to explain the facts in this case on my client's behalf; the judge will guide you and advise you on the correct interpretation of the law and you will then consider your verdict." "Unfortunately," Pakenham went on, "for reasons which I won't go into now, my grasp of the facts is not as it might be. The judge is nearing senility; his knowledge of the law is pathetically out of date, and will be of no use in assisting you to reach a verdict. While, by the look of you, the possibility of your reaching a coherent verdict can be excluded." He was led from the court.' – *THE DAILY TELEGRAPH*

SMOKERS RULE

Actor George Burns, famed for his love of fine cigars, was a long-time member of the exclusive Hillcrest Country Club in Los Angeles. When Burns complained one day about the club's new ban on smoking, a sign was promptly posted for the comedian's benefit: 'Cigar smoking prohibited for anyone under ninety-five.'

TOP TIPS FOR NOT GROWING OLD

'The best way to adjust – no, ignore – most of the negative thoughts about ageing is to say to yourself, with conviction, "I am still the very same person I have been all of my adult life." You are, you know. '– HELEN HAYES, ACTRESS

'If you rest, you rust.' – HELEN HAYES, ACTRESS

'If you don't want to get old, hang yourself while young.'
– JEWISH PROVERB

'Old minds are like old horses; you must exercise them if you wish to keep them in working order.' – JOHN QUINCY ADAMS, FORMER PRESIDENT

'Humour keeps the elderly rolling along, singing a song. When you laugh, it's an involuntary explosion of the lungs. The lungs need to replenish themselves with oxygen. So you laugh, you breathe, the blood runs, and everything is circulating. If you don't laugh, you'll die.' – MEL BROOKS, ACTOR AND PRODUCER

'You're never too old to become younger.' – Mae West, ACTRESS

'If you think nobody cares whether you are alive or dead, try missing a couple of car payments.' – Ann Landers, ADVICE COLUMNIST

'Never pass a bathroom.' – The Duke of Edinburgh

'You can't turn back the clock, but you can wind it up again.' – Bonnie Prudden, FITNESS GURU

'Look at everything as though you were seeing it either for the first or last time. Then your time on earth will be filled with glory.' – Betty Smith, WRITER

'Age puzzles me. I thought it was a quiet time. My seventies were interesting and fairly serene, but my eighties are passionate. I grow more intense as I age.' – Florida Scott-Maxwell, WRITER

'The older you get, the more important it is not to act your age.' – Ashleigh Ellwood Brilliant, WRITER AND CARTOONIST

'Let me advise thee not to talk of thyself as being old. There is something in Mind Cure, after all, and, if thee continually talk of thyself as being old, thee may perhaps bring on some of the infirmities of age.' – Hannah Whitall Smith, LAY SPEAKER AND WRITER

'Wig wearers! Secure your toupee in high winds by wearing a brightly coloured party hat with elasticated chin strap. Carry a balloon and a bottle of wine, and you'll pass off as an innocent party-goer.' – F. FINE-FARE, *VIZ*

'There is a fountain of youth: it is your mind, your talents, the creativity you bring to your life and to the lives of the people you love.' – SOPHIA LOREN, ACTRESS

'Use your health, even to the point of wearing yourself out. That is what it is for. Spend all you have before you die; do not outlive yourself.' – GEORGE BERNARD SHAW, PLAYWRIGHT

'If, by the time we are sixty, we haven't learned what a knot of paradox and contradiction life is, and how exquisitely the good and bad are mingled in every action we take, we haven't grown old to much purpose.' – JOHN COWPER POWYS, WRITER AND PHILOSOPHER

'An inordinate passion for pleasure is the secret of remaining young.' – OSCAR WILDE, WRITER

'Be careful about reading health books. You may die of a misprint.' – MARK TWAIN, WRITER

'The ageing process has you firmly in its grasp if you never get the urge to throw a snowball.' – DOUG LARSON, CARTOONIST

'One thing I've learned as I get older is just to go ahead and do it. It's much easier to apologize after something's been done than to get permission ahead of time.' – GRACE MURRAY HOPPER, REAR ADMIRAL AND EARLY COMPUTER PIONEER

'I have only managed to live so long by carrying no hatreds.' – WINSTON CHURCHILL, FORMER PRIME MINISTER

'Always keep tubes of haemorrhoid ointment and Deep Heat rub well separated in your bathroom cabinet.' – P. TURNER, *VIZ*

'No one should grow old who isn't ready to appear ridiculous.' – JOHN MORTIMER, WRITER AND DRAMATIST

 'Above all, don't be over-impressed by time. Accept it, but don't kowtow to it ... we should still be able to stick two fingers in the air as the diminishing amount of sand trickles through the hourglass.' – GEORGE MELLY, JAZZ SINGER

'We don't stop playing because we grow old, we grow old because we stop playing.' – GEORGE BERNARD SHAW, PLAYWRIGHT

'Don't ever save anything for a special occasion. Being alive is a special occasion.' – AVRIL SLOE

'One of the secrets of a long and fruitful life is to forgive everybody everything every night before you go to bed.' – BERNARD MANNES BARUCH, STATESMAN AND FINANCIER

'The secret to old age: you have to know what you're going to do the next day.' – LOUIS J. LEFKOWITZ, FORMER ATTORNEY GENERAL OF NEW YORK

'You are young at any age if you are planning for tomorrow. I take inspiration from that wonderful Scottish actor Finlay Currie. Shortly before he died at the age of ninety, he was asked on a TV chat show if he'd ever played a romantic lead. "Not yet, laddie," he replied. "Not yet."' – BOB MONKHOUSE, COMEDIAN

 'Bored? Here's a way the over-fifty set can easily kill a good half hour. 1) Place your car keys in your right hand. 2) With your left hand, call a friend and confirm a lunch or dinner date. 3) Hang up the phone. 4) Now look for your car keys.' – STEVE MARTIN, ACTOR AND COMEDIAN

'Whenever I'm confused, I just check my underwear. It holds the answer to all the important questions.' – GRAMPA SIMPSON, *THE SIMPSONS*

'Live well, learn plenty, laugh often, love much.' – RALPH WALDO EMERSON, ESSAYIST

'You stay young as long as you can learn, acquire new habits and suffer contradictions.' – MARIE VON EBNER-ESCHENBACH, WRITER

'I have studied many philosophers and many cats. The wisdom of cats is infinitely superior.' – HIPPOLYTE TAINE, FRENCH CRITIC AND HISTORIAN

'As I grow older, I pay less attention to what men say. I just watch what they do.' – ANDREW CARNEGIE, BUSINESSMAN AND PHILANTHROPIST

'It's never too late to be what you might have been.' – GEORGE ELIOT, WRITER

'If you're given the choice between money and sex appeal, take the money. As you get older, the money will become your sex appeal.' – KATHARINE HEPBURN, ACTRESS

A ROSE BY ANY OTHER NAME

Two elderly men, Ernest and Philip, are having lunch together, when Ernest turns to his friend and says, 'My wife and I went to a wonderful restaurant last night.'

'What was it called?' asks Philip, noticing the sudden look of confusion clouding his friend's face.

'What's the name of that flower that women like to get?' asks Ernest.

'A carnation?' suggests Philip.

'No.' Ernest frowns and looks thoughtful, before adding, 'It's red and has big petals.'

'Poppy?'

'No. It has a thorny stem.'

'Oh,' Philip nods, 'you mean a rose?'

'That's it.' Rising from his chair, Ernest wanders over to the staircase and shouts upstairs, 'ROSE! What's the name of that restaurant we went to last night?'

WHAT THE DOCTOR ORDERED?

A seventy-five-year-old man goes to the doctor to get a physical and a few days later the doctor sees him walking down the street with a stunning young lady on his arm and a huge smile on his face.

A couple more days pass and the old man returns to the doctor's surgery. After he has again examined the elderly man, the doctor writes him out a prescription and says, 'You're really doing great, aren't you?' The patient replies, 'Just doing what you said, Doctor: "Get a hot mamma and be cheerful." That's what you told me and that's what I've done.'

'Actually I said, "You've got a heart murmur, and be careful." Now, while you're here, why don't we check your hearing . . . ?'

PRACTICAL IDEAS TO KEEP THE MIND IN SHAPE AND SENIOR MOMENTS AT BAY

Given that everyone is prone to suffering senior moments, it is incredibly fortunate that there are so many ways in which we can, if not eradicate the problem entirely, then at least keep it at bay. Below are a few simple ideas on how to keep those mental faculties in tip-top shape:

Crosswords are an excellent form of mental gymnastics, provided that you can a) find where you last put down your glasses and b) find the newspaper. Studies have shown that people who do crossword puzzles four days per week had a 48 per cent lower risk of developing dementia than those who did no crosswords at all. That said, how about this revelation from a Guardian reader:

'I am eighty and have just done a parachute jump. Beats crosswords any day (though I do complete the Bunthorne Cryptic when I have time).' – J.W. MEPHAM, KINGSTON ON THAMES, SURREY

Take up chess, bridge or other games in which one has to plan out moves in advance in order to win. Large jigsaw puzzles are also good memory boosters since they require you to remember the precise shape and colour of hundreds of individual pieces. Or, if none of these takes your fancy, how about the following piece of advice from Cicero: 'To keep my memory in working order I repeat in the evening whatever I have said, heard, or done in the course of each day. These are the exercises of the intellect, these the training grounds of the mind: while I sweat and labour on these I don't feel much the loss of bodily strength.' – ON OLD AGE

Painting is yet another marvellous way to keep the mind active and the soul replenished. Young and old alike can partake in this activity, but the concentration required is especially helpful to those who are beginning to lose the ability to think clearly. Planning out your painting, choosing the type of paints you want to use, the required brushes for the effect you wish to create, your colour palette – all of these things exercise your mental faculties. Winston Churchill was a firm believer in this pursuit:

'One by one the more vigorous sports and exacting games fall away. Exceptional exertions are purchased only by a more pronounced and more prolonged fatigue. Muscles may relax, and feet and hands slow down; the nerve of youth and manhood may become less trusty. But painting is a friend who makes no undue demands, excites no exhausting pursuits, keeps faithful pace even with feeble steps, and holds her canvas as a screen between us and the envious eyes of Time or the surly advance of Decrepitude. Happy are the painters, for they shall not be lonely. Light and colour, peace and hope, will keep company to the end, or almost to the end of the day.' – QUOTED IN CHURCHILL, A PHOTOGRAPHIC PORTRAIT, BY MARTIN GILBERT

Never, ever, under any circumstance, allow yourself to be photographed. An unflattering snapshot can set your self-esteem back several centuries.

Try to avoid being herded into categories such as 'over-forties' or 'over-fifties'. It is never good for the ego to mix with large numbers of people the same age as you.

Yoga is an excellent activity for anyone experiencing the first aches and pains of seniordom. This ancient art not only helps to maintain a supple body, it will also nurture both mind and spirit, aiding with relaxation and rejuvenation. A word of warning, however, for those of you who have never practised yoga before: make sure you attend a beginner's class rather than trying to teach yourself out of a book, as some of the poses can leave you in very awkward positions!

BRIDGE

'Good sex is like good bridge. If you don't have a good partner, you'd better have a good hand.' – MAE WEST, ACTRESS

Bridge is an excellent tried-and-tested way to fend off senior moments. Studies have demonstrated that the game improves the memory, keeps players socially active and even helps to strengthen the immune system. As it is a game that can be played at multiple different levels and with a number of other players, it encourages healthy competition and a high degree of social interaction. Try putting time aside each week to join a bridge club, a perfect opportunity to get to grips with the game, develop your skills and meet like-minded people; or alternatively, why not organize bridge sessions within the comfort of your own home? Even if your body is no longer up to contact sports, bridge is a thoroughly satisfying and challenging alternative.

Medical research backs up the claim that bridge has beneficial physiological effects. According to a study carried out at the University of California, bridge players are more likely to live longer and look younger than people who do not play the game.

'Even as the hand is dealt, your immune system swings into action. The very sight of cards affects the frontal lobe of the brain, the thymus gland stimulates the T lymphocytes and after several long rubbers the dorsolateral cortex is so excited that your body can fend off almost any disease.' – THE TIMES, 'THE BRIDGE OF LIFE', NOVEMBER 2000

LOVE BITES

An elderly couple are lying in bed one night. Turning to her husband, the wife asks, 'Do you remember when we first started dating and you used to hold my hand?' Her husband leans over unenthusiastically and takes hold of his wife's hand before trying to get back to sleep.

A few moments later she says, 'Do you remember our first kiss? You used to kiss me all the time.' Mildly irritated, her husband reaches across, gives his wife a quick peck on the cheek and settles down to sleep.

Thirty seconds later his wife pipes up, 'Then you used to bite my neck.'

Angrily, her husband throws back the duvet, clambers out of bed and storms out of the room.

'Where are you going?' she calls after him.

'To get my teeth!'

ON THE INDIGNITIES OF AGE

At some time after 1955, when Sir Winston Churchill was in his eighties and had ceded the premiership to Eden, but remained a Member of Parliament, the politician was sitting in an armchair in the Members' Bar of the House of Commons. He was alone. Three young Tory MPs entered and, failing to see the old boy slouched in his armchair, began to chatter loudly. It soon became clear that the Member for Epping was the subject of their talk.

'You know,' one remarked, 'it's very sad about old Winston. He's getting awfully forgetful.'

'Shame, isn't it?' said another. 'He's really very doddery now, I gather.'

'Not only that,' added the third, 'but I've heard that he's going a bit – you know – gaga.'

'Yesh,' rumbled a deep voice from the nearby armchair, 'an' they shay he'sh getting terribly deaf, as well!'

FORGETFUL, MOI?

'How is it that our memory is good enough to retain the least triviality that happens to us, and yet not good enough to recollect how often we have told it to the same person?'
– Duc De La Rochefoucauld, writer

'Looking for one's pipe, then realizing it's in one's mouth, or for one's specs, pushed back on top of one's head. That can happen to anyone. But again and again – looking up foreign words in bilingual dictionaries, English/French, English/German, in the wrong half of the book . . . What is distinctly worse, I tell myself "dictionary", I must look up some word in the dictionary, to check on spelling or pronunciation. When I arrive at the word, I gaze at it uncomprehendingly: it is "dictionary".' – D. J. Enright, *Play Resumed: A Journal*

'I have another friend, a feminist, who, like me, is a member of the Voluntary Euthanasia Society. But she has forgotten all about it now that she is beginning to lose her mind. She has been on television and radio saying how she has helped people to die. She was knocked down by a car, made a wonderful recovery, and has never talked about euthanasia since.' – ROSE HACKER, *THE TIME OF YOUR LIFE*, COMPILED BY JOHN BURNINGHAM

SEEING RED

Two elderly women, Bessie and Eva, are out driving in a car and neither can see over the dashboard. Bessie is at the wheel and Eva is in the passenger seat. As they are cruising along, the car arrives at an intersection. The traffic light is red but Bessie drives straight through. Eva thinks to herself, 'I must be losing it, I could have sworn we just went through a red light.'

After a few more minutes they come to another intersection. The light is again set to red and again they drive straight through. This time, Eva is almost sure that the light was red, but she is also concerned that she might be seeing things. Looking nervously over at her companion, she decides to pay very close attention at the next set of lights.

When the car approaches the next intersection the light is definitely red and Bessie drives straight through it for a third time. Turning to her friend, Eva says, 'Bessie! Do you know we just ran through three red lights in a row? You could have killed us.'

Eva turns to her companion and asks, 'Oh dear, am I driving?'

MOTHER SUPERIOR – A SEVENTEENTH-CENTURY NUN'S PRAYER

Lord, Thou knowest better than I know myself, that I am growing older and will someday be old. Keep me from the fatal habit of thinking I must say something on every subject and on every occasion. Release me from craving to straighten out everybody's affairs. Make me thoughtful but not moody; helpful but not bossy. With my vast store of wisdom, it seems a pity not to use it all, but Thou knowest Lord that I want a few friends at the end.

Keep my mind free from the recital of endless details; give me wings to get to the point. Seal my lips on my aches and pains. They are increasing, and love of rehearsing them is becoming sweeter as the years go by.

I dare not ask for grace enough to enjoy the tales of others' pains, but help me to endure them with patience. I dare not ask for improved memory, but for a growing humility and a lessening cock-sureness when my memory seems to clash with the memories of others. Teach me the glorious lesson that occasionally I may be mistaken.

Keep me reasonably sweet; I do not want to be a Saint – some of them are so hard to live with – but a sour old person is one of the crowning works of the Devil. Give me the ability to see good things in unexpected places, and talents in unexpected people. And, give me, O Lord, the grace to tell them so.

Amen

AGE BEFORE BEAUTY

'Twenty-four years ago, madam, I was incredibly handsome. The remains of it are still visible through the rifts of time. I was so handsome that women became spellbound. In San Francisco, in rainy seasons, I was frequently mistaken for a cloudless day.'
– MARK TWAIN, WRITER

'Keep looking at my eyes, dahling. My ass is like an accordion.'
– TALLULAH BANKHEAD, ACTRESS

'Alas, after a certain age every man is responsible for his face.'
– ALBERT CAMUS, WRITER AND PHILOSOPHER

'Ageing gracefully is supposed to mean trying not to hide time passing and just looking a wreck. That's what they call ageing gracefully. You know? Don't worry girls, look like a wreck, that's the way it goes. You suffer when you give birth . . . Don't take care of yourself because you want to stop time – do it for self-respect. It's an incredible gift, the energy of life. You don't have to be a wreck. One's aim in life should be to die in good health.'
– JEANNE MOREAU, ACTRESS

'I have the body of an eighteen-year-old. I keep it in the fridge.'
– SPIKE MILLIGAN, COMEDIAN AND WRITER

'Things for guys to consider before buying a hairpiece: will it appreciate in value? Is it possible a hairpiece will make me look too good? Will I be able to handle all the women? Have I explored all my combover options?' – DAVID LETTERMAN, TALK-SHOW HOST

'Talk about getting old. I was getting dressed and a peeping tom looked in the window, took a look and pulled down the shade.'
– JOAN RIVERS, COMEDIAN

'Women are not forgiven for ageing. Robert Redford's lines of distinction are my old-age wrinkles.' – JANE FONDA, ACTRESS

'When I go upstairs my buttocks applaud me and my knees sound like potato chips.' – JOAN RIVERS, COMEDIAN

'I said to my husband, "My boobs have gone, my stomach's gone – say something nice about my legs." He said, "Blue goes with everything."' – JOAN RIVERS, COMEDIAN

'Cut off my head and I am thirteen.' – COCO CHANEL, COUTURIER

'I knew I was going bald when it was taking longer and longer to wash my face.' – HARRY HILL, COMEDIAN

'So much has been said and sung of beautiful young girls, why don't somebody wake up to the beauty of old women?'
– HARRIET BEECHER STOWE, WRITER

'Is there anything worn under the kilt?
No, it's all in perfect working order.'
– SPIKE MILLIGAN, COMEDIAN AND WRITER

'I think your whole life shows in your face and you should be proud of that.'
– LAUREN BACALL, ACTRESS

SENIOR SYMPHONY

One evening while attending one of George Gershwin's parties, Groucho Marx was approached by a fellow guest.

'Do you think Gershwin's melodies will be played a hundred years from now?' he asked.

'Sure,' Groucho replied, 'if George is here to play them.'

CATALOGUE OF COMPLAINTS

A group of senior citizens are discussing their various ailments in a nursing home one afternoon.

'I am so feeble that I can hardly lift this cup of coffee,' says one old lady.

'Tell me about it, my cataracts are so bad I can't even see what's on my plate,' replies another.

'I can't turn my head because of the arthritis in my neck.'

'My joints are so stiff and swollen that I have difficulty getting up to go to the bathroom at night.'

'Well, at least you're not incontinent, like me.'

'My blood-pressure pills make me dizzy,' another old lady continues, and several people nod in sympathetic agreement.

'I guess that's the price you pay for getting old,' sighs one old gentleman, slowly shaking his head.

'Well, it's not that bad,' said one woman cheerfully, 'at least we can still drive.'

ANNABEL'S STORY

Mother of three, Annabel, having been pestered to death by her children for a pet, finally cracked and acquired a loveable rabbit named Fred. Fred was docile, soft and fluffy, came fully house-trained, and was content to hop peacefully around Annabel's house and garden. In short, Fred was everything you would want from a rabbit.

The honeymoon period was soon over. One day, whilst attempting to feed her ten-month-old baby with one hand, defrost a loaf of bread in the oven with the other, and prevent Fred from chewing through some wiring near the floor, Annabel scooped the pesky rabbit up, unceremoniously dumped him in his cage, bunged the bread in the oven and continued unfazed.

Several minutes later, another of her children, Alice, appeared, to query tearfully why was there a loaf of bread in Fred's cage? And where was Fred?

At this point Annabel's entire life flashed before her eyes and she began to suffer olfactory hallucinations as her nostrils filled with the sweet odour of roasted rabbit. To her utter amazement her son Hamish then ran into the kitchen with Fred, totally unharmed, under his arm. Crying tears of relief, Annabel hugged first her son, then her daughter. When she was sufficiently calm, Annabel remembered the oven: if it wasn't Fred in there, who or what was?

Gingerly, she opened the oven door, only to be greeted by a cloud of black smoke and the charred remains of a single fluffy slipper.

TENDER MEMORY

A man walks into a bar and has a couple of beers. When he is finished the barman tells him that he owes £6.00.

'But I already paid, don't you remember?' asks the customer.

'Okay,' the barman agrees. 'If you say you paid, you paid.' The man goes outside and tells the first person he sees that the barman can't keep track of whether his customers have paid or not. The second man then rushes in, orders a beer and later tries the same trick. The bartender this time replies, 'If you say you paid, I'll take your word for it.'

The customer then goes into the street, sees an old friend and tells him how to get free drinks. The man hurries into the bar, orders three pints and begins to drink rapidly, when suddenly the bartender leans over and says, 'You know, a strange thing happened in here this afternoon. Two men were drinking beer, neither paid and both claimed that they did. The next person who tries that is going to regret it.'

'I'm sorry to hear that,' the final patron replies. 'Just give me my change and I'll be on my way.'

SAY WHAT?

Two elderly women are eating breakfast one morning when one of them notices something funny about her friend's ear.

'Mildred, do you know you've got a suppository in your left ear?'

'Do I really? A suppository?' Mildred pulls it out and stares at it.

'Ethel, I'm glad you saw this thing. Now I know where my hearing aid is.'

BODILY FUNCTIONS

Apart from a failing memory, nothing is as guaranteed as the body to bring on a senior moment. Just picture the scene: you're in the prime of life, playing a game of tennis, when suddenly your left knee gives way and, hey presto, you're no longer sprinting nimbly about the court like a budding Lleyton Hewitt, but being carried off it on a stretcher. Another common scenario: at forty-five years of age, you don't see anything untoward about taking out the rubbish, that is until you bend to pick it up and give yourself a hernia. Or, how about that moment when you're watching TV and suddenly all those ads for anti-wrinkle cream become more world-shatteringly important than listening to the state of the economy, global warming, or the onset of World War III?

Now, instead of having upper arms, you have to suffer the indignity of 'bingo wings' or 'Hi Bettys', i.e. those indiscreet bits of flesh that wobble whenever you lift your arms to wave or attract someone's attention. Nor does the suffering stop there. Stomachs, outer thighs, inner thighs, double chins, triple chins – the number of ways in which your body can let you down are too numerous and ghastly to mention. Everything you took for granted about your body when you were a teenager or in your twenties or thirties has shrunk, drooped or simply gone AWOL. Gypsy Rose Lee spoke for senior citizens everywhere when she remarked: 'I have everything now that I had twenty years ago, except now it's all lower.'

Here are some other observations on youth's departure:

'Your face is not so much lived in as, like the late Robert Maxwell's, taken over by squatters. Your fatty tissue feels like overripe grouse, like the flesh of an old whore marinated in a bidet. The hairs in your nose sprout as if you've been sniffing Grow More, and the struggle to cut your toenails becomes an epic to match War and Peace. Your body has a mind of its own. And your mind seems to be running out of your ears, like the sands of time. You have accumulated a wealth of experience, but you have forgotten what it is.' – PIERS BRENDON, THE TIME OF YOUR LIFE, COMPILED BY JOHN BURNINGHAM

'Capsules for incipient ulcer. Impossible to open the damned container. Is one that feeble? "Created sick, commanded to be sound." Incipient ulcer grows more incipient. "How To Open": the incomprehensible diagram on the cap resembles the stylized matchstick figures in an illustrated edition of the Kama Sutra that once came my way. This seems odd, considering what care for our well-being, what awareness of our stupidity, manufacturers so often show. A pack of sleeping pills carries the warning, "May cause drowsiness"; on a packet of peanuts, "Contains nuts"; attached to a common domestic appliance, "Do not iron clothes on body."'
– D. J. ENRIGHT, PLAY RESUMED: A JOURNAL, 1999

'I was under the care of a couple of students who couldn't diagnose a decapitation.'
– JEFFREY BERNARD, JOURNALIST

'When you get to my age, life seems little more than one long march to and from the lavatory.' – JOHN MORTIMER, WRITER AND DRAMATIST

'I don't need you to remind me of my age. I have a bladder to do that for me.' – STEPHEN FRY, COMEDIAN AND ACTOR

'I reach the age of sixty. Until about five years ago I detected no decline at all in physical vigour and felt as young as I did at thirty. In the last five years, however, I am conscious that my physical powers are on the decline. I am getting slightly deaf and the passions of the flesh are spent.' – HAROLD NICOLSON, *HAROLD NICOLSON DIARIES AND LETTERS 1930-1964*

'There's nothing wrong with you that an expensive operation can't prolong.' – GRAHAM CHAPMAN, COMEDIAN AND WRITER

'I'm at an age where my back goes out more than I do.' – PHYLLIS DILLER, COMEDIAN

'Growing old brings some disadvantages, like you start having trouble with the coconut ones in Liquorice Allsorts; bending over becomes a major decision; and you can't count the number of times a day you find yourself moving in one direction when you should be moving in the other.' – DENIS NORDEN, COMEDIAN AND TV PRESENTER

'You don't know real embarrassment until your hip sets off a metal detector.' – ROSS MCGUINESS

'When I wake up in the morning and nothing hurts, I know I must be dead.' – GEORGE BURNS, ACTOR AND WRITER

'You're fifty years old! Can they make a drug to help you through all of that, to keep all your organs intact until your golden years? No. Can they make a drug to give mental clarity to your golden time? No. What they've got is Viagra, a drug to make you harder than Chinese algebra.' – ROBIN WILLIAMS, ACTOR AND COMEDIAN

'I visited a new dentist for my six-monthly check-up. Having given me the all-clear, he glanced at my notes, then remarked: "Those should see you out."' – ANGELA WALDER

'Thanks to modern medical advances such as antibiotics, nasal spray and Diet Coke, it has become routine for people in the civilized world to pass the age of forty, sometimes more than once.' – DAVE BARRY, WRITER AND COMEDIAN

'My granny wore a hearing aid that was always tuned too low. Because when she turned it up, it whistled, and every dog in Dublin rushed to her side.'
– TERRY WOGAN, RADIO AND TV BROADCASTER

FREE-FALLING

During the filming of the 1998 thriller, Crazy Six, Burt Reynolds was determined to do his own stunts. 'Look, I can do this. I can still fall,' he told the film's producers. 'I just can't get up.'

REGRETS – I'VE HAD A FEW

'I rather regret I haven't taken more drugs. Is it too late, at seventy, to try cocaine? Would it be dangerous or interesting?' – JOAN BAKEWELL, JOURNALIST AND TV PRESENTER

'The only thing in my life that I regret is that I once saved David Frost from drowning. I had to pull him out, otherwise nobody would have believed I didn't push him in.' – PETER COOK, COMEDIAN

'If I had my life to live over, I'd live over a saloon.'
– W.C. FIELDS, COMEDIAN AND ACTOR

MORE ANCIENT WORDS OF WISDOM . . .

'But you may urge – there is not the same tingling sensation of pleasure in old men. No doubt; but neither do they miss it so much. For nothing gives you uneasiness which you do not miss. That was a fine answer of Sophocles to a man who asked him when in extreme old age, whether he was still a lover. "Heaven forbid!" he replied. "I was only too glad to escape from that, as though from a boorish and insane master."To men indeed who are keen after such things it may positively appear disagreeable and uncomfortable to be without them: to the jaded appetites it is pleasanter far to lack than to enjoy. However, he cannot be said to lack who does not want: my contention is that not to want is the pleasantest thing.' – CICERO, ON OLD AGE

. . . AND A FEW MODERN WORDS OF CONFUSION

'Left for work yesterday, family all gone on school run, incensed by the mess left by the dustmen, had to lean bicycle up against the wall and clear up mess, pick up lids and overturned bins etc., muttering under breath etc., growling at small children passing on their way to school etc., get on bike, go to work. Get to work – telephone call from wife – "You left the front door open!"' – ANON

A DOUBLE LIFE

American comedian and entertainer Jack Benny often claimed to be thirty-nine years old. So it was fitting that Frank Sinatra's gift to Benny on his eightieth birthday was two copies of *Life Begins at 40*.

SOCKS

No other item of clothing is as troublesome to the senior citizen as the sock. It would not be far-fetched to think that this sartorial creation was a cosmic joke aimed at those over sixty.

Socks look snug and feel soft, they offer warmth and comfort; they are seemingly the perfect companion for us in our old age. Do not be fooled. Socks don't just disappear in washing machines or inexplicably get lost somewhere between the tumble-dryer and our sock drawers. No, they are also set to taunt us as we grow older, so that attempting to put on a pair of these little blighters becomes an Olympic sport in itself.

'The time will come in your life, it will almost certainly come, when the voice of God will thunder at you from a cloud, "From this day forth thou shalt not be able to put on thine own socks." To the young, to the middle-aged, even, this may seem a remote and improbable accident that only happens to other people. It has to be said, however, that the day will most probably dawn when your pale foot will wander through the air, incapable of hitting the narrow opening of a suspended sock. Those fortunate enough to live with families will call out for help. The situation is, in minor ways, humiliating and comical.' – JOHN MORTIMER, *THE SUMMER OF A DORMOUSE*

THREE LADIES

Three sisters aged sixty-five, seventy-five and seventy-seven years old all live together in the same house. The eldest sister goes upstairs to run a bath, puts her foot in the water, then shouts out,'Was I getting out of this bath or getting in?'

The middle sister, who has been sitting downstairs reading a newspaper, gets up to help. She starts climbing the stairs, but then shouts out, 'Hey, am I coming down the stairs or going up them?'

The youngest sister, who has been drinking tea in the kitchen, lets out an enormous sigh and mutters under her breath, 'God, I hope I never get that forgetful,' knocking on wood for good measure.

'Okay,' she shouts out, 'I'll be up in a minute to help sort you out – I've just got to see who's at the door.'

HOT UNDER THE COLLAR

Thirty-five-year-old Samantha lived in Melbourne and had two children, as well as a tendency to acute hypochondria. She was always suffering from some terrible disease. When she had a cold it was pneumonia, when she had a headache it was a brain tumour, a stomach ache was often said to be appendicitis. So when, for no apparent reason, Samantha began experiencing memory loss, suddenly she was convinced she was going through the menopause.

'It is the menopause,' she would shriek at anyone who cared to listen. 'I forgot to pick the children up from nursery school yesterday. The car's never where I parked it – I don't know whether I'm coming or going.'

Eventually Samantha took herself off to her doctor and insisted he ran some tests, all of which proved negative. Samantha wasn't going through 'the change'; she was just getting a little forgetful like we all do occasionally.

Dissatisfied with her doctor's diagnosis, Samantha continued to insist that she was exhibiting all the classic symptoms of the menopause. At every given opportunity she would regale her sister with tales of hot flushes, insomnia, memory and concentration problems, until one day the two of them were sitting in Samantha's kitchen having a chat.

Standing up to make some tea, while continuing to talk to her sister about something one of her children had done the previous afternoon, Samantha suddenly put her hand to her forehead before proceeding to fan herself frantically, much to Beryl's amusement.

'You see! You see!' she shouted melodramatically, so that her two children came tumbling downstairs. 'I'm having a hot flush right now. Look at me!'

Her sister simply smiled calmly and opened the window.

'Sam,' she said, 'The kettle's boiled.'

MENOPAUSAL MOMENTS

Senior moments and menopausal moments can overlap to such an extent that women often think they really are going mad. To spot the latter as opposed to the former, here are a few helpful hints:

Your darling husband starts joking that instead of installing a new wood-burning stove this winter, he is going to use you to keep the family warm. Instead of laughing heartily at his joke, you shoot him.

You start writing Post-It notes with your children's names on them – and even then you stick them to the wrong child.

The medication you have been prescribed by your doctor – you know the one – that bottle of little white pills that helped wipe out the Heaven's Gate cult, allows you to get at least three hours' sleep per night.

MENOPAUSAL QUOTES

'A friend of mine, Norma Cowles, started The Change at Pontins in Torquay, but there were absolutely no menopausal facilities there whatsoever. Something for Judith Chalmers to think about.'
– MRS MERTON, *THE MRS MERTON SHOW*

'It's the menopause. I've got my own climate.'
– JULIE WALTERS, ACTRESS

'My grandma told me, "The good news is, after the menopause the hair on your legs gets really thin and you don't have to shave any more. Which is great because it means you have more time to work on your new moustache."' – KAREN HABER, WRITER

'Why did the menopausal woman cross the road? To kill the chicken.' – JANE CONDON, COMEDIAN

'I'm trying very hard to understand the younger generation. They have adjusted the timetable for childbearing so that menopause and teaching a sixteen-year-old how to drive a car will occur in the same week.' – ERMA BOMBECK, NEWSPAPER COLUMNIST

'The menopause is the stage that a woman goes through when her body, through a complex biological process, senses that the woman had reached the stage in her life where her furniture is much too nice for her to have a baby barfing on it.' – DAVE BARRY, WRITER AND COMEDIAN

IF YOU DON'T MOVE IT, YOU LOSE IT

Keeping our bodies active is as important as feeding ourselves the right food. If we don't want to suffer the indignity of not being able to put on our own socks or tie our own shoelaces, particular attention should be paid to our everyday exercise routines, in order that the ageing process can be slowed down. A brisk half-hour walk once or twice a week is a good way to begin building up stamina. Swimming is also an excellent way to keep your body in shape as, during your time in the pool, you will be exercising your entire musculoskeletal system.

Exercise is a wonderful way to increase our happiness, as endorphins, which help to fight against depression, are released by the brain during periods of high activity. Sports such as tennis, ping-pong, volleyball and badminton not only help with our hand/eye coordination, but they are also great at relieving stress, as the degree of concentration required means that all your other worries are forgotten.

'I cannot describe to you how I felt fourteen or fifteen miles into the thing [the London Marathon], the Old Un having left me at thirteen miles when I started walking. Here I was, the youngest of Team Oldie, enviously eyeing those people being carted off in wheelchairs and wondering if they would mind if I sat on their laps.'
– JIM TRANTER, '*RUN IT BEFORE YOU SNUFF IT*', *THE OLDIE*

'I am getting to an age when I can enjoy only the last sport left. It is called hunting for your spectacles.' – LORD GREY OF FALLODON, *THE OBSERVER*

'You gotta keep in shape. My grandmother started walking five miles a day when she was sixty. She's ninety-seven today and we don't know where the hell she is.' – ELLEN DEGENERES, ACTRESS AND COMEDIAN

'Health nuts are going to feel stupid someday, lying in hospitals dying of nothing.' – REDD FOXX, COMEDIAN

'To get back my youth, I would do anything in the world, except take exercise, get up early, or be respectable.' – OSCAR WILDE, PLAYWRIGHT AND NOVELIST

'Exercise is bunk. If you are healthy, you don't need it: if you are sick, you should not take it.' – HENRY FORD, AUTOMOBILE MANUFACTURER

'I'm not feeling very well – I need a doctor immediately. Ring the nearest golf course.' – GROUCHO MARX, COMEDIAN AND ACTOR

'I'd like to learn to ski, but I'm forty-four and I'm worried about my knees. They creak a lot and I'm afraid they might start an avalanche.' – JONATHAN ROSS, TV AND RADIO PRESENTER

'I exercise every morning without fail. Up, down! Up, down! And then the other eyelid.' – PHYLLIS DILLER, COMEDIAN

'I am pushing sixty. That is enough exercise for me.'
– MARK TWAIN, WRITER

'I keep fit. Every morning I do 100 laps of an Olympic-sized swimming pool – in a small motor launch.' – PETER COOK, COMEDIAN

'I now realize that the small hills you see on ski slopes are formed around the bodies of forty-seven-year-olds who tried to learn snowboarding.' – DAVE BARRY, WRITER AND COMEDIAN

'Police in Norway stopped Sigrid Krohn de Lange running down the street in Bergen because they thought that she had escaped from a nursing home. The ninety-four-year-old jogger was out getting fit.' – THE IRISH INDEPENDENT

NB: Do not undertake any new form of exercise without first consulting your doctor.

ONE-TRACK MIND

On his eighty-ninth birthday, the French conductor Pierre Monteux was interviewed by the BBC. 'I still have two abiding passions,' he declared. 'One is my model railway, the other women. But at the age of eighty-nine, I find I am getting just a little too old . . . for model railways.'

OPEN-AND-SHUT CASE

When quizzed on how he retained his youthful appearance into his seventies, American entertainer Dick Clark replied, 'I keep an open mind . . . and a closed refrigerator.'

MALAPROPISMS

Another sure sign that senior moments are upon you is that age-old affliction known as the malapropism. Suddenly, or so it seems, our brains cannot cope with placing words in the right order or, for that matter, using the correct word in the correct place. Of course, the word comes originally from Mrs Malaprop, a character in Richard Sheridan's play, The Rivals, written in 1775. Here are a few of her more famous verbal contortions:

MRS MALAPROPISMS

'O, he will dissolve my mystery!'

'His is the very pineapple of politeness.'

' . . . promise to forget this fellow – to illiterate him, I say, quite from your memory.'

'I hope you will represent her to the captain as an object not altogether illegible.'

'Oh! it gives me the hydrostatics to such a degree.'

'I have since laid Sir Anthony's preposition before her.'

'I am sorry to say, Sir Anthony, that my affluence over my niece is very small.'

'She's as headstrong as an allegory on the banks of the Nile.'

'Why, murder's the matter! Slaughter's the matter! Killing's the matter! – but he can tell you the perpendiculars.'

' . . . behold, this very day, I have interceded another letter from the fellow.'

'I thought she had persisted from corresponding with him.'

' . . . she might reprehend the true meaning of what she is saying.'

'Your being Sir Anthony's son, captain, would itself be a sufficient accommodation.'

'I am sorry to say, she seems resolved to decline every particule that I enjoin her.'

' . . . if ever you betray what you are entrusted with . . . you forfeit my malevolence for ever . . . '

'Sure, if I reprehend any thing in this world it is the use of my oracular tongue, and a nice derangement of epitaphs!'

MORE MALAPROPISMS

'Barbara, didn't Elsie next door have implants?'
'No, eggplants, Mam.' – *THE ROYLE FAMILY*

'We seem to have unleased a hornet's nest.' – VALERIE SINGLETON,
TV PRESENTER

'My nan was complaining of chest pains. I said, "Are you all right,
Nan?" She said, "I think I've got vagina."' – PETER KAY, COMEDIAN

'My mum said, "I saw whatsaname last week, oh, whatshisname,
I can never remember anything these days – it's this damned
anorexia."' – STEPHEN FRY, COMEDIAN AND ACTOR

'This is unparalyzed in the state's history.' – GIB LEWIS, TEXAS SPEAKER
OF THE HOUSE

'He's on ninety . . . ten away from that mythical figure.'
– TREVOR BAILEY, CRICKET COMMENTATOR

'Marie Scott . . . has really plummeted to the top.' – ALAN WEEKS,
SPORTS COMMENTATOR

'My nan, God bless 'er, gets things a bit mixed up. She said to
me the other day, "I've bought one of those new George Formby
grills."' – PETER KAY, COMEDIAN

'Unless somebody can pull a miracle out of the fire, Somerset are cruising into the semi-final.' – FRED TRUEMAN, CRICKETER

'This series has been swings and pendulums all the way through.' – TREVOR BAILEY, CRICKET COMMENTATOR

'The police are not here to create disorder, they're here to preserve disorder.' – RICHARD J. DALEY, FORMER CHICAGO MAYOR

'He was a man of great statue.' – THOMAS M. MENINO, BOSTON MAYOR

'If Gower had stopped that [cricket ball] he would have decapitated his hand.' – FAROKH ENGINEER, FORMER CRICKETER

FATHER WILLIAM

In Lewis Carroll's novel *Alice's Adventures in Wonderland* (1865), the writer parodies Robert Southey's 'The Old Man's Comforts' (1799), which begins:

> 'You are old, Father William,' the young man cried,
> 'The few locks which are left you are grey;
> You are hale, Father William, a hearty old man,
> Now tell me the reason, I pray.'

Southey's poem focuses on how God rewards in old age those who do not forget Him in youth. Carroll's poem takes a lighthearted and whimsical look at old age:

> 'You are old, Father William,' the young man said,
> 'And your hair has become very white;
> And yet you incessantly stand on your head –
> Do you think, at your age, it is right?'

> 'In my youth,' Father William replied to his son,
> 'I feared it might injure the brain;
> But now that I'm perfectly sure I have none,
> Why, I do it again and again.'

> 'You are old,' said the youth, 'as I mentioned before,
> And have grown most uncommonly fat;
> Yet you turned a back somersault in at the door –
> Pray, what is the reason of that?'

'In my youth,' said the sage, as he shook his grey locks,
'I kept all my limbs very supple
By the use of this ointment – one shilling the box –
Allow me to sell you a couple.'

'You are old,' said the youth, 'and your jaws are too weak
For anything tougher than suet;
Yet you finished the goose, with the bones and the beak –
Pray, how did you manage to do it?'

'In my youth,' said his father, 'I took to the law,
And argued each case with my wife,
And the muscular strength which it gave to my jaw
Has lasted the rest of my life.'

'You are old,' said the youth, 'one would hardly suppose
That your eye was as steady as ever;
Yet you balanced an eel on the end of your nose –
What made you so awfully clever?'

'I have answered three questions, and that is enough,'
Said his father; 'Don't give yourself airs!
Do you think I can listen all day to this stuff?
Be off, or I'll kick you downstairs!'

FOREVER YOUNG

'The secret of staying young is to live honestly, eat slowly, and lie about your age.' – LUCILLE BALL, ACTRESS

'My recipe for perpetual youth? I've never had my face in the sun, and I have a very handsome young husband . . . Sex is one of the best and cheapest beauty treatments there is.' – JOAN COLLINS, ACTRESS AND WRITER

'Youth is a wonderful thing. What a crime to waste it on children.' – GEORGE BERNARD SHAW, WRITER

'My health is good; it's my age that's bad.' – RAY ACUFF, COUNTRY MUSIC SINGER

'I wish I was a twin, so I could know what I'd look like without plastic surgery.' – JOAN RIVERS, COMEDIAN

'I call them the lizard women. They're the ones who have had so much cosmetic surgery that they're no longer biodegradable. They look like giant Komodo dragons with Chanel accessories.' – BRETT BUTLER, COMEDIAN

'Now I'm getting older I take health supplements: geranium, dandelion, passionflower, hibiscus. I feel great, and when I pee, I experience the fresh scent of pot pourri.' – SHEILA WENZ

'I don't plan to grow old gracefully. I plan to have facelifts until my ears meet.' – RITA RUDNER, COMEDIAN AND WRITER

'How does one keep from "growing old inside"? Surely only in community. The only way to make friends with time is to stay friends with people . . . Taking community seriously not only gives us the companionship we need, it also relieves us of the notion that we are indispensable.' – ROBERT MCAFEE BROWN

'Old Father Time will turn you into a hag if you don't show the bitch who's boss.' – MAE WEST, ACTRESS

'How foolish to think that one can ever slam the door in the face of age. Much wiser to be polite and gracious and ask him to lunch in advance.' – NOEL COWARD, ACTOR AND PLAYWRIGHT

GARDENS OF DELIGHT

Senior moments occur in all shapes and sizes, but they are often brought on by the stressful, hectic pace of modern life. If we aren't rushing to work, we're rushing to pick up the children or grandchildren. We try and meet up with friends, only to get stuck in a traffic jam. We go for a walk and our mobile phones start to ring. We seek sanctuary in a church and someone else's mobile starts buzzing. There is no escape from it all. Small wonder, then, that our brains start to malfunction and cause us to forget whether we're coming or going. But don't panic – there is a solution at hand: gardening.

Apart from booking yourself into a Cistercian monastery for a couple of months, there is no better way to relax the mind and rejuvenate the spirit than getting in touch with the earth. Who cares if you can't recall the names of your plants or how frequently they should be watered, pruned, mulched or composted? Does it really matter if you dig up flowers, plant weeds and can't remember where you put all those precious seeds you collected last year? The fact that you are outside and getting acquainted with nature should be enough to stave off any number of senior moments, and give you enormous pleasure into the bargain.

'I perceive that they are planting oaks on the "wastes", as the Agriculturasses call them, about Hartley Row . . . The planter here is Lady Mildmay, who is, it seems, Lady of the Manors about here. It is impossible to praise this act of hers too much, especially when one considers her age. I beg a thousand pardons! I do not mean to say that Her Ladyship is old; but she has long had grandchildren. If Her Ladyship had been a reader of old dread-death and dread-devil

Johnson, that teacher of moping and melancholy, she never would have planted an oak tree.' – WILLIAM COBBETT, RURAL RIDES

'The gardener's rule applies to youth and age: When young sow wild oats, but when old grow sage.' – LORD BYRON, POET

'Gather ye rosebuds while ye may,
Old Time is still a-flying
And this same flower that smiles today,
Tomorrow will be dying.'
– ROBERT HERRICK, 'TO THE VIRGINS, TO MAKE MUCH OF TIME'

'God gave us memories, so that we might have roses in December.'
– JAMES MATTHEW BARRIE, WRITER AND DRAMATIST

'I am spending delightful afternoons in my garden, watching everything living around me. As I grow older, I feel everything departing, and I love everything with more passion.' – EMILE ZOLA, WRITER

WEATHER OR NOT

Three retired gentlemen, each with bad hearing, are playing golf on a blustery afternoon. One remarks to the other, 'Windy, isn't it?'

'No,' the second man replies, 'it's Thursday.' And the third man chimes in, 'So am I. There's a pub just round the corner.'

MIDDLE AGE

'The most frightening thing about middle age is that you'll grow out of it.' – DORIS DAY, SINGER AND ACTRESS

'Enjoy yourself, it's later than you think.' – CHINESE PROVERB

'Middle age is the awkward period when Father Time starts catching up with Mother Nature.' – HAROLD COFFIN, JOURNALIST

'Middle age: becoming like our parents while fighting with our children.' – ELLIOT PRIEST

'As someone said recently of the Rolling Stones, "They're not a rock band any more, but a handful of middle-aged men acting as a rock band." And we are a few thousand middle-aged geeks, acting as an audience. The experience compares, in its excrutiatingness, to the time I went  to a Bob Dylan concert with a philosophy professor who did not smoke, but had brought a lighter especially, to wave in the dark.' – KATE MUIR, *THE TIMES*

'Middle age is when anything new in the way you feel is most likely a symptom.' – SIDNEY BODY

'Wisdom doesn't always show up with age. Sometimes age shows up all by itself.' – TOM WILSON, CARTOONIST

'Of all the barbarous middle ages, that which is most barbarous is the middle age of man.' – LORD BYRON, POET

'Growing old – it's not nice but it's interesting.' – AUGUST STRINDBERG, WRITER

'Middle age: when the past was perfect, and the present is tense.' – ELLIOT PRIEST

'Middle age is the best time, if we can escape the fatty degeneration of the conscience which often sets about at fifty.' – W.R. INGE, WRITER AND ANGLICAN PRELATE

'At middle age the soul should be opening up like a rose, not closing up like a cabbage.' – JOHN ANDREW HOLMES

'Men are okay from thirty to forty-five; if they're careful they can stay about the same. After that it's an increasing struggle because of jowl and neck lines, even if the waist can be restrained. And the bruising of repeated sexual rejection starts to show in the eyes.' – ALAN CLARKE, DIARIES

'I remember being shocked when I met an ex-student I used to teach and she told me she was thirty! She must have left nine years ago! A little later I became used to bumping into greying, balding, fat old men at parties, who turned out to be ex-students. They were in their forties and unrecognizable. Lately, one or two have come crawling out in their fifties!' – RAYMOND BRIGGS, *THE TIME OF YOUR LIFE*, COMPILED BY JOHN BURNINGHAM

REBECCA'S STORY

Everyone enjoys going on holiday, and for Rebecca, her four-week stay in Australia was going to be the holiday of a lifetime. She spent months choosing exactly where she was going, booking the flights and hotel, buying new clothes, having her legs and bikini line waxed, checking her passport was up to date, booking her animals into a pet hotel, leaving instructions for her friends, who were going to stay in her house while she was away; in short, she had done everything and anything she could think of to ensure that her holiday would run like clockwork.

On the morning of her departure, Rebecca woke up with her alarm, showered, pulled on her clothes and then waited for the taxi, which she had booked the previous evening. Everything was running without a hitch. The taxi driver arrived and duly deposited her at Heathrow airport (albeit with a smirk on his face), where she unloaded her bags on to a trolley and began pushing them towards the check-in desk.

At this stage, Rebecca began to notice that people were looking at her a bit strangely. With a cold shiver running up her spine, she looked down at what she was wearing. In her eagerness to get to the airport, instead of donning her holiday clothes, Rebecca had, for some reason known only to the deep recesses of her subconscious, gotten back into her nightie, dressing gown and slippers.

She was standing in the middle of Heathrow airport, all decked out for bed.

HOLDING BACK THE YEARS

A lady goes into a cosmetics shop to buy a new anti-ageing face cream which, according to the advert, is 'guaranteed' to make the years drop off. Following the instructions carefully, she religiously applies just the right amount twice a day, and waits expectantly for the results.

After a few weeks, she decides that it's time to see if her husband has noticed any difference. One evening before bed she plucks up the courage to ask him.

'Darling, tell me the truth, what age would you say I am?'

Looking her up and down, her husband replies, 'Well, Susan, judging from your skin – twenty; your hair – eighteen; and your figure – twenty-five.'

'Oh, you flatterer!' she gushes, before kissing him.

'Hey, wait a minute,' he interrupts, 'I haven't added them up yet.'

OVER THE HILL?

So there you are, skipping along life's uneven path,when suddenly a young whippersnapper comes along to trip you up by pointing out that you are not only over the hill, but tumbling down the other side. It is invariably those younger than yourself who seem to think they have a God-given right to point this fact out. Indeed, the cult of youth is almost single-handedly responsible for giving old age an image akin to that of the plague. In former centuries, those members of an older generation were regarded as sages and philosophers to look up to and respect. Nowadays, quite the opposite is true, with the general consensus being that if you aren't in your teens or early twenties, you might as well order your coffin now and be done with it. And, if you don't believe it, take a look at the following quotes:

'I can't wait until I'm thirty and I give up modelling because I'll be wrinkly and my bottom will be sagging . . . ' – JODIE KIDD, *DAILY MAIL*

'Discussing the forthcoming contest to fill the gap that will be left on the Today programme when Sue McGregor steps down as a presenter, the editor Rod Liddle commented: "It would be nice to have a few people under forty with a bit of edge to them."' – *NEW STATESMAN*

'The sight of an old woman [Joan Collins] still apparently believing that self-esteem depends on looking good and having a man is profoundly depressing, not to mention exhausting.' – FRANCES TAYLOR, *THE TIMES*

'Grey-haired men look "distinguished"? Surely the word is "extinguished".' – JULIE BURCHILL, JOURNALIST

'Two years ago I was at a lakeside trying to negotiate a speedboat ride for my daughter and two of my nieces. The man I was haggling with quoted an outrageous price. Taken by surprise, I said, "How much?"

"What's the matter, Pops," he said, "losing your hearing also?"

"Pops? POPS! Do I look like a Pops?" I thought. "And what does he mean by 'also'?"
I bent over and, Narcissus style, looked at my reflection in the water. He was right. Peter Pan was nowhere to be seen. Sardonic middle age looked up at me from the water. You are getting old, Father William.' – ELIAKIM KATZ, WRITER

'His toupee makes him look twenty years sillier.' – BILL DANA, NEW STATESMAN

'I went on a Saturday to visit Syon House, the Duke of Northumberland's stately home beside the Thames in Middlesex. As I asked for an entrance ticket, the woman behind the counter said, "Are you an adult?" I was initially flattered that she appeared to be uncertain whether I had yet passed the age of puberty, but then I realized what she was on about. She wanted to know if I was still an adult – in other words, whether or not I had passed from adulthood into dotage.' – ALEXANDER CHANCELLOR, THE GUARDIAN

'Here is proof that no one makes the case for natural boobs better than Madonna … She may be getting on a bit . . . ' – THE SUN

'There aren't many actors of [Michael Caine's] vintage who are playing parts which suggest that the life force is still very much intact, without humiliating themselves by agreeing to be presented as romantic leads for actresses half their age.' – *THE TIMES MAGAZINE*

'He [Edward Fox] may be sixty-eight, but apart from the deep valleys and crevices in his stern, craggy face, there is no suggestion that he has "gone off".' – SHOLTO BYRNES, JOURNALIST

'The invite for Top of the Pops reads: "Over-18s but no wrinklies". Most of the audience weren't even born the last time David Cassidy was famous. Any older fans that do get into the studio will have their grey heads edited out of the broadcast.' – NICK CURTIS, *EVENING STANDARD*

'She [Catherine Zeta-Jones] looks like Sophia Loren on steroids.' – SUSANNAH CONSTANTINE, TV PRESENTER

'Sex and the City star Kim Cattrall has complained that she is finding it hard to get a date. Well, dear, it's what you should expect … As we get older we all begin to have difficulty with dates, names, where we parked . . . ' – *THE SUNDAY TIMES*

'Jockey Mick Kinane is in his fifth year at the County Tipperary stable and has played a full part in the unparalleled success of trainer Aidan O'Brien. At forty-four, however, there are those who feel his strongest and sharpest days are behind him.' – *THE TIMES*

'At Salisbury Magistrates' Court, Margaret Phelps, sixty-one, pleaded guilty to harassing David Conio, a sixty-two-year-old removal man. She sent him love letters, bottles of whisky and played Elvis Presley's "Love Me Tender" down the phone. After Phelps was given a twelve-month community rehabilitation order and a twelve-month restraining order, Mr Conio commented: "You expect that sort of behaviour from a young, besotted teenager who has been turned down in the love stakes, but not from a sixty-two-year-old woman."' – *THE TIMES*

'Paula Rego ... is on the cusp of proper old age. Ahead of her are the years of terminality. And were she really one of ours,we would expect her to begin taking the weight off her feet round about now, to sink back in her armchair and embark on an inner life of rumination and yearning, regret and silence. Her anger ought to be turning into melancholy. And sex – one of her favourite motor forces – ought to be becoming a memory rather than a growing hazard.' –WALDEMAR JANUSZCZAK, *THE SUNDAY TIMES*

'If you register with the electronic Daily Telegraph, you must give your date of birth; if you were born before January 1, 1920, you have to lie, as this is the earliest you are allowed to have been born. Obviously the paper deems everyone over eighty-one either not worth bothering about or incapable of surfing the net.' – STEPHANIE JENKINS, AS QUOTED IN *NOT DEAD YET*

'In the end, whether men of a certain age run off with one woman half our age or twenty women twice our age, whether we leave home to spend our Saturday nights emptying our wallets into the thongs of exotic dancers in a strip palace in Wichita County, or our Sunday mornings weeping through coffee concerts at the Wigmore Hall, it all comes down to the melancholy of being a man, and the further melancholy of being a man in what we now have to call "late middle age" because we cannot bear to use the word "old".' – HOWARD JACOBSON, *EVENING STANDARD*

'She may have reached thirty, but Cameron Diaz has a figure that would be the envy of women half her age.' – *NOW* MAGAZINE

'The phone rang. "We are doing a survey about use of the internet.
   May I ask you some questions?"
   "Yes."
   "First of all, how old are you?"
   "Sixty-nine."
   "You're too old. Thank you for your time. Goodbye."'
– TONY GREENFIELD, AS QUOTED IN *NOT DEAD YET*

'I get to meet a lot of really neat older people. Women who are, like,
thirty.' – AMANDA BYNES, ACTRESS AND TV PRESENTER

'Harrison Ford, with his ear stud and inappropriately younger
partner, Calista Flockhart, needs someone to slap him round the
face with an order of sushi before he falls too deeply into the theatre
of the male menopause.' – TIM LOTT, *EVENING STANDARD*

'People I work with say, "You're an old woman. My God! Get
your slippers back on." All I ever want is a game of Scrabble.'
– KYLIE MINOGUE, SINGER

'"Aren't you beginning to feel your age?" I ask fifty-year-old
Michael Palin.' – CASSANDRA JARDINE, *THE DAILY TELEGRAPH*

'The only reason Patricia Hewitt, the minister of e-commerce, is not
already in the Cabinet is that she left it rather late to be elected an
MP – she was forty-eight when she entered the Commons in 1997.'
– *THE DAILY TELEGRAPH*

'Police in Sun City West, Arizona, have logged more than two dozen complaints in a year of couples having sexual intercourse at swimming pools, car parks and on public benches. The average age of the perpetrators being seventy-three . . . ' – *EVENING STANDARD*

'Sophia Loren, despite her age, was recently voted the most beautiful woman in the world.' – *THE INDEPENDENT*

'From the Evening Standard: "But Riding's real problem is that, unlike her co-stars Jonathan Pryce and Dennis Waterman, she is primarily a creature of the theatre. At thirty-four, her looks, frankly, get better the cheaper the seat you are in." Poor actress Joanna Riding! Only thirty-four and the reviewer Andrew Billen can't bear to sit close to her.' – *SASKIA VAN DER LINDEN, EXTRACT FROM NOT DEAD YET*

OUT OF ORDER

Every now and then our brains go on the blink to the extent that it might be just as well to pin an 'Out of Order' sign on our foreheads. Strangely, sports commentators are a breed particularly susceptible to the sort of mental blips that result in malapropisms. Whether it is a result of the fast pace of delivery required to keep up with the action, or the sheer excitement of bearing witness to feats of sporting prowess, there is no arguing that the sports commentator frequently speaks before he thinks. Next time you forget to think before you speak, just thank God you're not broadcasting live to the nation . . .

'José Mourinho has got the Midas touch right now – everything he touches turns to silver.' – RICHARD KEYS, *SKY SPORTS*

'I thought we started very, very brightly, but then the Achilles heel which has bitten us in the backside all year has stood out like a sore thumb.' – ANDY KING

'And the crowd go wild as they see the shaven head of Hagler enter the auditorium. And there he is, hooded . . . ' – REG GUTTERIDGE, BOXING COMMENTATOR

'It's a unique occasion, really – a repeat of Melbourne 1977.' – JIM LAKER, CRICKETER AND SPORTS

'I owe a lot to my parents, especially my mother and father.'
– GREG NORMAN, GOLFER

'A brain scan revealed that Andrew Caddick is not suffering from stress fracture of the shin.' – JO SHELDON, *SKY NEWS*

'Boycott, somewhat a creature of habit, likes exactly the sort of food he himself prefers.' – DON MOSEY, RADIO PRODUCER AND SPORTS COMMENTATOR

'I never comment on referees and I'm not going to break the habit of a lifetime for that prat.' – RON ATKINSON, FORMER FOOTBALLER AND MANAGER

'Sure there have been injuries and deaths in boxing – but none of them was serious.' – ALAN MINTER, FORMER BOXER AND WORLD MIDDLEWEIGHT CHAMPION

'Both these players seem to anticipate the play of the other almost before it's happened.' – TONY GUBBA, SPORTS COMMENTATOR

'Bradford, who had gone up from 200 metres to 400, found it hard going and for the last 100 was always going backwards.'
– DAVID COLEMAN, SPORTS COMMENTATOR

'I have other irons in the fire, but I'm keeping them close to my chest.' – JOHN BOND, FORMER FOOTBALLER AND MANAGER

'History, as John Bond would agree, is all about todays and not about yesterdays.' – BRIAN MOORE, SPORTS COMMENTATOR

' . . . and he has lit a fuse to a match that was already boiling.'
– ALAN PARRY

'Even when you're dead you shouldn't lie down and let yourself be buried.' – GORDON LEE, FORMER FOOTBALLER AND MANAGER

'And here's Moses Kiptanui – the nineteen-year-old Kenyan, who turned twenty a few weeks ago.' – DAVID COLEMAN, SPORTS COMMENTATOR

'Ah! Isn't that nice, the wife of the Cambridge President is kissing the cox of the Oxford crew.' – HARRY CARPENTER, SPORTS COMMENTATOR

'Playing with wingers is more effective against European sides like Brazil than English sides like Wales.'
– RON GREENWOOD, FORMER ENGLAND
FOOTBALL MANAGER

'We now have exactly the same situation as we had at the start of the race, only exactly the opposite.' – MURRAY WALKER, MOTOR-RACING COMMENTATOR

'Fred Davis, the doyen of snooker, now sixty-seven years of age and too old to get his leg over, prefers to use his left hand.'
– TED LOWE, SNOOKER COMMENTATOR

AGE DEFIES GRAVITY

One evening late in his life, former senator Chauncey Depew found himself seated at a dinner party beside a young woman in a low-cut, off-the-shoulder dress. Looking the scantily clad woman over, the senator leaned in towards her.

'My dear,' he asked, 'what is keeping that dress on you?' The woman's reply?

'Only your age, Mr Depew!'

THE TIME OF YOUR LIFE

'Write, paint, sculpt, learn the piano, take up dancing, whether it's the tango or line dancing, start a college course, fall in love all over again – the possibilities are limitless for you to achieve your private ambitions.' – JOAN COLLINS, ACTRESS AND WRITER

'You're never too old. A person of sixty can grow as much as a child of six. Michelangelo did some of his best paintings when past eighty; George Bernard Shaw was still writing plays at ninety; Grandma Moses didn't even begin painting until she was seventy-nine.' – MAXWELL MALTZ, COSMETIC SURGEON AND WRITER

'Every man desires to live long but no man would be old.'
– Jonathan Swift, '*Thoughts on Various Subjects*'

'Look, I don't want to wax philosophic, but I will say that if you're alive you've got to flap your arms and legs, you've got to jump around a lot, for life is the very opposite of death, and therefore you must at the very least think noisily and colourfully, or you're not alive.' – Mel Brooks, actor and producer

'When you're young, you don't know, but you don't know you don't know, so you take some chances. In your twenties and thirties, you don't know, and you know you don't know, and that tends to freeze you; less risk taking. In your forties you know, but you don't know you know, so you may still be a little tentative. But then, as you pass fifty, if you've been paying attention, you know, and you know you know. Time for some fun.' – George Carlin, comedian

'Develop interest in life as you see it: in people, things, literature, music – the world is so rich, simply throbbing with treasures, beautiful souls and interesting people. Forget yourself.'
– Henry Miller, writer

'I can't actually see myself putting make-up on my face at the age of sixty. But I can see myself going on a camel train to Samarkand.'
– Glenda Jackson, actress and politician

'I am more alive than most people. I am an electric eel in a pond of goldfish.'
– Edith Sitwell, poet and critic

FORGET ME NOT

An eighty-five-year-old man marries a beautiful twenty-two-year-old woman. Because her husband is so old, his bride decides that on their wedding night they should sleep in separate beds. The last thing she wants is for him to overexert himself on their first night together as man and wife.

After the wedding the young lady gets ready for bed, climbs under the covers and waits expectantly. Sure enough, she hears a knock. The door opens, and there stands her husband, ready for action. When they have finished making love, the old man leaves and his young wife prepares to sleep.

A few minutes pass before the woman is awoken by another knock on her bedroom door. Surprised to find her husband there again, she lets him in and is astonished by his sexual prowess. When they are finished, the old man kisses his wife, bids her goodnight and leaves.

Exhausted by this time, the young woman is ready to go to sleep again. However, after a space of just a few minutes, there follows another knock at her door and there stands the groom again, as fresh as a twenty-five-year-old and ready for a bit more action.

When he is once again set to leave, his bride turns to him and says, 'I'm amazed, sweetheart. I've been with men a quarter of your age who were good only once! You're a fantastic lover.'

Somewhat embarrassed, the old man scratches his head, turns to his wife and says, 'You mean I've been here already?'

SENIOR STATESMEN PART I

Forgetfulness and repeating oneself aren't just confined to the everyday man on the street. Anyone over the age of thirty, be they social worker or statesman, can fall foul to these debilitating afflictions. Take, for example, British Prime Minister Tony Blair. When the Labour party leader pronounced that his top policy was 'Education, education, education', those of us over the age of thirty-five realized he wasn't doing so for effect, but that the poor old fool had simply forgotten what it was he'd said only seconds before.

Many other politicians, particularly those on the other side of the pond, could be accused, if not of repeating themselves, then of making absolutely no sense at all. From Ronald Reagan and Dan Quayle to Donald Rumsfeld and George Bush (both Senior and Junior), American politicians have peppered their speeches with malapropisms worthy of Mrs Malaprop herself. As senior moments go, the following selection of quotations borders on the sublime:

GEORGE BUSHISMS

'Somebody – somebody asked me, what's it take to win? I said to them, I can't remember, what does it take to win the Super Bowl? Or maybe Steinbrenner, my friend George, will tell us what it takes for the Yanks to win – one run. But I went over to the Strawberry Festival this morning, and ate a piece of shortcake over there – able to enjoy it right away – and once I completed it – it didn't have to be approved by Congress, I just went ahead and ate it – and that leads me into what I want to talk to you about today.'

'Ours is a great state and we don't like limits of any kind. Ricky Clunn is one of the great bass fishermen. He's a Texas young guy, and he's a very competitive fisherman, and he talked about learning to fish wading in the creeks behind his dad. He, in his underwear, went wading in the creeks behind his father, and he said – as a fisherman – he said it's great to grow up with no limits.'

'I think I've got to do better in making clear what the message is, and I think I can do better. But I think there's so much noise out there that I've got to figure out how to make it clearer that we are for the things that I have advocated that would help.'

GEORGE W. BUSHISMS

'I know how hard it is for you to put food on your family.'

'The Holocaust was an obscene period in our nation's history. I mean in this century's history. But we all lived in this century. I didn't live in this century.'

'It's clearly a budget. It's got a lot of numbers in it.'

'Listen, Al Gore is a very tough opponent. He is the incumbent. He represents the incumbency. And a challenger is somebody who generally comes from the pack and wins, if you're going to win. And that's where I'm coming from.'

'Anyway, I'm so thankful, and so gracious – I'm gracious that my brother Jeb is concerned about the hemisphere as well.'

'There's no question that the minute I got elected, the storm clouds on the horizon were getting nearly directly overhead.'

'The fact that he relies on facts – says things that are not factual – are going to undermine his campaign.'

'Laura and I really don't realize how bright our children is sometimes, until we get an objective analysis.'

'I think we agree, the past is over.'

'If the East Timorians decide to revolt, I'm sure I'll have a statement.'

'The administration I'll bring is a group of men and women who are focused on what's best for America, honest men and women, decent men and women, women who will see service to our country as a great privilege and who will not stain the house.'

'For every fatal shooting, there were roughly three non-fatal shootings. And, folks, this is unacceptable in America. It's just unacceptable. And we're going to do something about it.'

'I have made good judgements in the past. I have made good judgements in the future.'

'I don't think we need to be subliminable about the differences between our views on prescription drugs.'

'That's a chapter, the last chapter of the twentieth, twentieth, twenty-first century that most of us would rather forget. The last chapter of the twentieth century. This is the first chapter of the twenty-first century.'

'This is Preservation Month. I appreciate preservation. It's what you do when you run for president. You gotta preserve.' – SPEECH DURING 'PERSEVERANCE MONTH'

'I suspect that had my dad not been president, he'd be asking the same questions: How'd your meeting go with so-and-so? . . . How did you feel when you stood up in front of the people for the State of the Union Address . . . State of the Budget Address . . . whatever you call it.'

'This administration is doing everything we can to end the stalemate in an efficient way. We're making the right decisions to bring the solution to an end.'

'There's a huge trust. I see it all the time when people come up to me and say, "I don't want you to let me down again."'

'It isn't pollution that's harming the environment. It's the impurities in our air and water that are doing it.'

'They said, "You know this issue doesn't seem to resignate with the people." And I said, "You know something? Whether it resignates or not doesn't matter to me, because I stand for doing what's the right thing, and what the right thing is, is hearing the voices of people who work."'

'I am mindful not only of preserving executive powers for myself, but for predecessors as well.'

'I want it to be said that the Bush administration was a results-orientated administration, because I believe the results of focusing our attention and energy on teaching children to read and having an education system that's responsive to the child and to the parents, as opposed to mired in a system that refuses to change, will make America what we want it to be – a more literate and a hopefuller country.'

'If you're sick and tired of the politics of cynicism and polls and principles, come and join this campaign.'

Governor Bush: 'I have talked to my little brother, Jeb – I haven't told this to many people. But he's the governor of – I shouldn't call him my little brother – my brother, Jeb, the great governor of Texas. Florida.'
Jim Lehrer: 'Florida.'
Governor Bush: 'Florida. The state of the Florida.'

'You teach a child to read, and he or her will be able to pass a literacy test.'

'Quite frankly, teachers are the only profession that teach our children.'

VERY OLD TESTAMENT

Next time some insensitive youth tells you that you are getting on a bit, or that you're over the hill, you have one foot in the grave, or you're past your sell-by date etc., think upon the remarkable feats and deeds of those Old Testament characters who gave a whole new meaning to the expression 'to have a good innings'. Here are just a few examples:

Adam: The Book of Genesis states that 'And all the days that Adam lived were nine hundred and thirty years: and he died' (5:5). Adam also fathered his first son, Seth, at the age of 130. Seth obviously inherited his father's sturdy genes, living to the remarkable age of 912, and begetting numerous sons and daughters along the way.

Methuselah: The oldest person mentioned in the Bible, Methuselah reportedly reached the age of 969. According to the Book of Genesis, 'And all the days of Methuselah were nine hundred sixty and nine years: and he died' (5:27). Methuselah was the father of Enoch and Lamech, whom he fathered at the age of 187.

Moses: As if it wasn't enough that he led the Israelites out of Egypt and then nipped up Mount Sinai to receive the Ten Commandments, Moses went on to live to the impressive age of 120. According to the Book of Deuteronomy, 'And Moses was an hundred and twenty years old when he died: his eye was not dim, nor his natural force abated' (34:7). As a result, the expression 'May you live to 120' is common blessing among Jews.

Kohath: Kohath was a son of the Jewish patriarch and leader of the priesthood, Levi, and his wife Melcha. The Book of Exodus says little about Kohath except that he lived for 133 years and fathered four sons: Amram, Izhar, Hebron and Uzziel.

Abraham: Traditionally regarded as the father of the three major monotheistic religions – Judaism, Christianity and Islam – the great patriarch Abraham is said to have lived to the grand old age of 175 after a period spent in Egypt. His wife Sarah famously gave birth to their son Isaac in her old age, after a long period of sterility, and went on to live to the age of 127.

SHAKES-PEERING

When the poet and critic W. H. Auden arrived to deliver a lecture on Shakespeare at the New School for Social Research in New York, the poet was pleased to discover that every seat in the room had been filled.

'If there are any of you who do not hear me,' Auden began, looking at the sea of faces in the audience, 'please don't raise your hands, because I am also near sighted.'

GOLDEN OLDIES – SECRETS OF LONGEVITY

'To what do I attribute my longevity? Bad luck, mostly.' – BILLY WILDER, SCREENWRITER AND PRODUCER

'Scientists say that women who have children after forty are more likely to live to be 100, but they don't know why. I think the reason is, they're waiting for the day when their kids move out of the house.' – LORRIE MOSS

'To keep the heart unwrinkled, to be hopeful, kindly, cheerful, reverent – that is to triumph over old age.' – THOMAS BAILEY ALDRICH, POET AND WRITER

'Q. To what do you attribute your long life?
A. To the fact that I haven't died yet.'
– SIR MALCOLM SARGENT, CONDUCTOR AND COMPOSER

'The onset of senile dementia is very gradual and insidious. When the patient has some occupation where intellectual faculties are required, attention may be drawn to him earlier on account of some eccentric actions or sayings. Thus, a clergyman, instead of dismissing the congregation at the close of the sermon, may begin his discourse afresh and preach a second time. Comment is thus provoked, and attention drawn to the patient, when other little oddities are remembered, and a typical case of senile dementia is gradually made apparent. But, however first brought to notice, the earliest symptom is loss of memory.' – G. H. DOUDNEY, *MALADIES OF OLD AGE AND THEIR TREATMENT*

'Being an old maid is like death by drowning, a really delightful sensation once one ceases to struggle.' – EDNA FERBER, WRITER AND PLAYWRIGHT

'In spite of illness, in spite even of the arch-enemy sorrow, one can remain alive long past the usual date of disintegration if one is unafraid of change, insatiable in intellectual curiosity, interested in big things, and happy in a small way.' – EDITH WHARTON, WRITER

'Nobody grows old merely by living a number of years. We grow old by deserting our ideals. Years may wrinkle the skin, but to give up enthusiasm wrinkles the soul.' – SAMUEL ULLMAN, BUSINESSMAN AND POET

'Q. What is the secret of your long life?
A. Keep breathing.' – SOPHIE TUCKER, SINGER AND COMEDIAN

'Alcohol is good for you. My grandfather proved it irrevocably. He drank two quarts of booze every mature day of his life and lived to the age of 103. I was at the cremation – the fire would not go out.' – DAVE ASTOR, NEWSPAPER PUBLISHER

'At seventy, I'm in fine fettle for my age, sleep like a babe and feel around twelve. The secret? Lots of meat and cigarettes and not giving in to things.' – JENNIFER PATTERSON, JOURNALIST AND TV PRESENTER

'Q. Happy 103rd Birthday, Mr Zukor. What is the secret of your long life?
A. I gave up smoking two years ago.' – ADOLPH ZUKOR, FILM MOGUL

'The secret of my long life? Swim, dance a little, go to Paris every August, and live within walking distance of two hospitals.'
– DR HORATIO LURO, HORSE-RACING TRAINER

'Age is an issue of mind over matter. If you don't mind, it doesn't matter.' – MARK TWAIN, WRITER

THE FOUR SEASONS

'The course of life is fixed, and nature admits of its being run but in one way, and only once; and to each part of our life there is something seasonable; so that the feebleness of children, as well as the high spirit of youth, the soberness of maturer years, and the ripe wisdom of old age – all have a certain natural advantage which would be secured in its proper season.'
– CICERO, *ON OLD AGE*

LONG DIVISION

Upon the occasion of his turning eighty, American vaudeville singer Sophie Tucker's ex-husband informed her of a new development in his love life. The octogenarian allegedly rang up his former wife and said, 'Soph! Soph! I just married myself a twenty-year-old girl. What do you think of that?' Tucker's response swiftly followed. 'Ernie, when I am eighty I shall marry me a twenty-year-old boy. And let me tell you something, Ernie: twenty goes into eighty a helluva lot more than eighty goes into twenty!'

LIFE IS . . .

'Life is a moderately good play with a badly written third act.'
— Truman Capote, writer

'Life is a funny thing that happens to you on the way to the grave.'
— Quentin Crisp, writer and actor

'Life is available to anyone no matter what age. All you have to do is grab it.' – Art Carney, actor

'Life is a marathon in which you reserve the sprint for the end. Mentally I pace myself. I have got an energy bank account and I can't afford to be overdrawn.' – Peter Ustinov, writer and actor

'Life can only be understood backwards, but it must be lived forwards.' – Søren Kierkegaard, philosopher

'Life is rather like opening a tin of sardines. We're all of us looking for the key.' – Alan Bennett, writer and actor

'Life is too short, but it would be absolutely awful if it were too long.'
— Peter Ustinov, writer and actor

OLD AGE IS . . .

'Old age is remembering Cup Final teams and goals of generations past far more vividly than you can those of, well, only two days ago.'
– FRANK KEATING, POLITICIAN

'By the time we've made it, we've had it.' – MALCOLM FORBES, PUBLISHER OF *FORBES MAGAZINE*

'Old age is life's unsafe harbour.' – ELLIOTT PRIEST

'Old age equalizes – we are aware that what is happening to us has happened to untold numbers from the beginning of time. When we are young, we act as if we were the first young people in the world.'
– ERIC HOFFER, WRITER

'Age is a high price to pay for maturity.' – TOM STOPPARD, PLAYWRIGHT

'Growing old is mandatory; growing up is optional.' – CHILI DAVIS, FORMER BASEBALL PLAYER

'Old age is the most unexpected of all the things that happen to a man.' – LEON TROTSKY, REVOLUTIONARY

'As I grow older and older
And totter towards the tomb
I find that I care less and less
Who goes to bed with whom.'
– DOROTHY L. SAYERS, '*THAT'S WHY I NEVER READ MODERN NOVELS*', IN JANET HITCHMAN'S *SUCH A STRANGE LADY*

SILVER LININGS

'Q. You're eighty-six years old. You smoke ten cigars a day, drink five martinis a day, surround yourself with beautiful women. What does your doctor say about all this?

A. My doctor is dead.'

– GEORGE BURNS, ACTOR AND WRITER

'Good things about being the Oldest Person in the World: You make the Guinness World Records without doing a damn thing; at your 100th high-school reunion you've got the buffet all to yourself; you don't need denture cleaner – you can just call the grandchildren and borrow theirs; you can suck at golf and still shoot your age; you can smoke all you damn well please.'

– DAVID LETTERMAN, TALK-SHOW HOST

'I love having the freedom to do what I want, when I want and not care a darn what anyone else thinks. Like the old lady in Jenny Joseph's poem, "I shall spend my pension on brandy and summer gloves", and no one can stop me!' – LILLIAN HOWARD

'The happiness of finding idleness a duty. No more opinions, no more politics, no more practical tasks.'

– W. B. YEATS, POET AND DRAMATIST

'One of the signs of passing youth is the birth of a sense of fellowship with other human beings as we take our place among them.' – VIRGINIA WOOLF, WRITER

'People like you and I, though mortal of course like everyone else, do not grow old no matter how long we live . . . [We] never cease to stand like curious children before the great mystery into which we were born.' – ALBERT EINSTEIN, SCIENTIST

'How pleasant is the day when we give up striving to be young – or slender.' –WILLIAM JAMES, PSYCHOLOGIST AND PHILOSOPHER

'One pleasure attached to growing older is that many things seem to be growing younger; growing fresher and more lively than we once supposed them to be.' – G.K. CHESTERTON, WRITER

'I think happiness is easier to come by when you're older: go for a nice walk and do some push-ups. Sex is always good. A hamburger will work, if you make it right and make it yourself. It should be rare and have raw onion and a lot of mustard. A martini, just one, is really fabulous. Going to Mass on Sunday morning, if it is the right sort of Mass, if the homily is short and the choir hangs together just right . . . Sleep. Sleep is always good. You almost always feel better when you wake up. Baseball games. And Louis Armstrong . . . ' – GARRISON KEILLOR, WRITER AND COMEDIAN

'I always make a point of starting the day at 6 a.m. with champagne. It goes straight to the heart and cheers one up. White wine won't do. You need the bubbles.' – JOHN MORTIMER, WRITER AND DRAMATIST

'Wrinkles should merely indicate where smiles have been.' – MARK TWAIN, WRITER

'The spiritual eyesight improves as the physical eyesight declines.' – PLATO, PHILOSOPHER

'The great thing about getting older is that you don't lose all the other ages you've been.' – MADELEINE L'ENGLE, WRITER

'There is more felicity on the far side of baldness than young men can possibly imagine.' – LOGAN PEARSALL SMITH, WRITER

'Now I'm getting older, I don't need to do drugs any more. I can get the same effect just by standing up real fast.' – JONATHAN KATZ, COMEDIAN AND ACTOR

'No pleasure is worth giving up for the sake of two more years in a geriatric home in Weston-super-Mare.' – KINGSLEY AMIS, WRITER

'Give me chastity and continence, but not yet.' – SAINT AUGUSTINE

'These are the soul's changes. I don't believe in ageing. I believe in forever altering one's aspect to the sun. Hence my optimism.' – VIRGINIA WOOLF, WRITER

'One good thing about getting older is that if you're getting married, the phrase "Till death do us part" doesn't sound so horrible. It only means about ten or fifteen years and not the eternity it used to mean.' – JOY BEHAR, COMEDIAN AND TV PRESENTER

'The woman who has a gift for old age, is the woman who delights in comfort. If warmth is known as the blessing it is, if your bed, your bath, your best-liked food and drink are regarded as fresh delights, then you know how to thrive when old.' – FLORIDA SCOTT-MAXWELL, WRITER AND PLAYWRIGHT

'I advise you to go on living solely to enrage those who are paying your annuities. It is the only pleasure I have left. When I feel an attack of indigestion coming on, I picture two or three princes as gainers by my death, take courage out of spite, and conspire against them with rhubarb and temperance.' – VOLTAIRE, WRITER AND PHILOSOPHER

'I have enjoyed greatly the second blooming that comes when you finish the life of the emotions and of personal relations; and suddenly find – at the age of fifty, say – that a whole new life has opened before you, filled with things you can think about, study, or read about . . . It is as if a fresh sap of ideas and thoughts was rising in you.' – AGATHA CHRISTIE, WRITER

'The joy of being older is that in one's life one can, towards the end of the run, overact appallingly.' – QUENTIN CRISP, WRITER AND ACTOR

'Sometimes it's fun to sit in your garden and try to remember your dog's name.' – STEVE MARTIN, ACTOR AND COMEDIAN

'One of the advantages of being seventy is that you need only four hours' sleep. True, you need it four times a day, but still.' – DENIS NORDEN, COMEDIAN AND TV PRESENTER

'As you grow old, you lose your interest in sex, your friends drift away, your children often ignore you. There are many other advantages, of course, but these would seem to be the outstanding ones.' – RICHARD NEEDHAM, *TORONTO GLOBE AND MAIL*

'If I'm feeling really wild, I don't bother flossing before bedtime.' – JUDITH VIORST, PRESENTER

'All one's life as a young woman one is on show, people notice you. You set yourself up to be noticed and admired. And then, not expecting it, you become middle-aged and anonymous. No one notices you. You achieve a wonderful freedom. It is a positive thing. You can move about, unnoticed and invisible.' – DORIS LESSING, WRITER

'From fifty-one to fifty-three I have been happy, and would like to remind others that their turn can come, too. It is the only message worth giving.' – E.M. FORSTER, WRITER

'One positive thing about getting older is that you develop a sense of perspective about your legacy to future generations. People say things like, "We're going to use up our earth's resources. The earth will be uninhabitable by 2050." And I find myself nodding and going, "No problem, I'll be dead."' – DAVE BARRY, WRITER AND COMEDIAN

'Did you know that by the time he'd turned eighty, Winston Churchill had coronary thrombosis, three attacks of pneumonia, a hernia, two strokes and something known as a senile itch? All the same, though often setting fire to himself, he still managed to enjoy a cigar.' – BERYL BAINBRIDGE, WRITER

'During much of my life, I was anxious to be what someone else wanted me to be. Now I have given up that struggle. I am what I am.'
– ELIZABETH COATSWORTH, WRITER AND POET

'When it is dark enough, you can see the stars.'
– CHARLES A. BEARD, HISTORIAN

'A few perks of old age: things I buy now won't wear out; I enjoy hearing arguments about pensions; my secrets are safe with my friends because they can't remember them either.' – FELICITY MUIR

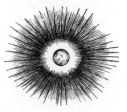

THE PRIME OF LIFE?

One day in his eighty-seventh year, Justice Oliver Wendell Holmes Jr. is rumoured to have passed a beautiful girl while out walking with an old friend. 'Oh,' he sighed, turning to watch her as she walked away, 'to be seventy again!'

OLD GIRLS' REUNION

When a studio usher knocked on the door of Ethel Barrymore's Hollywood dressing room and announced that there were a couple of girls hanging about outside who said they went to school with her, and enquired as to what he should do, Barrymore's reply came quickly: 'Wheel them in.'

LATE BLOOMERS

You are never too old to achieve your goals. Experience is a fine thing and it is never too late to see the world in new and different ways. Just take a look at the following senior success stories for inspiration:

George Burns won his first Oscar at the grand old age of eighty.

The author Mary Wesley, who wrote The Camomile Lawn, had her first novel published after the age of seventy.

At age fifty the philosopher Plotinus was persuaded by his students to write down his ideas, which were subsequently published as The Enneads.

Painter Grandma Moses painted her first picture when she was past eighty years old, completing over 1,500 paintings during the rest of her life.

Michelangelo was seventy-one when he painted the ceiling of the Sistine Chapel.

Physician and humanitarian Albert Schweitzer was still performing operations in his African hospital at the age of eighty-nine.

Marc Chagall, at the age of ninety, became the first living artist to be exhibited at the Louvre.

Pablo Picasso produced drawings and engravings into his nineties.

Italian sculptor, architect and painter Gian Lorenzo Bernini began designing churches aged sixty.

Physicist William Sturgeon created the first electromagnet at the age of forty.

Herman Hesse wrote Steppenwolf at the age of fifty.

SENIOR STATESMEN PART II

Ronald Reaganisms

'Trees cause more pollution than automobiles.'

'We're trying to get unemployment to go up, and I think we're going to succeed.'

'I have left orders to be awakened at any time in case of national emergency, even if I'm in a cabinet meeting.'

'I understand small-business growth. I was one.'

'It's evolutionary, going from governor to president, and this is a significant step, to be able to vote for yourself on the ballot, and I'll be able to do so next fall, I hope.'

Dan Quayleisms

'What a waste it is to lose one's mind. Or not to have a mind is being very wasteful. How true that is.'

'We don't want to go back to tomorrow, we want to go forward.'

'Actually, I – this may sound a little west Texan to you, but I like it. When I'm talking about – when I'm talking about myself, and when he's talking about myself, all of us are talking about me.'

'We are ready for any unforeseen event that may or may not occur.'

'Hawaii has always been a very pivotal role in the Pacific. It is in the Pacific. It is a part of the United States that is an island that is right here.'

Donald Rumsfeldisms

'Reports that say that something hasn't happened are always interesting to me, because as we know, there are known knowns; there are things we know we know. We also know there are known unknowns; that is to say, we know there are some things we do not know. But there are also unknown unknowns – the ones we don't know we don't know.'

'We do know, of certain knowledge, that [Osama Bin Laden] is either in Afghanistan or in some other country or dead.'

BARKING MAD

One sunny day in April, the Petunia family were in a state of great apprehension, for Auntie Tabatha was on her way over for tea. Tabatha,who was in her early fifties, did not suffer fools gladly, and had made herself greatly unpopular with the Petunias due to her stringent Victorian principles, expounded in the oft-repeated phrase 'Children ought to be seen and not heard'. Where other aunts and uncles brought sweeties and five-pound notes, Aunt Tabatha would repeat this phrase ad nauseam, glowering at the children from beneath her pencilled eyebrows. Eva Petunia had taken the usual and necessary precaution of warning the children to be on their very best behaviour.

Aunt Tabatha duly arrived and, catching sight of a dish on the sideboard full of biscuits, began to berate Eva for filling the children up with sugar and fat.

'It's not good for them, you know,' she said, frowning sternly, without giving her sister a chance to explain. 'They'll become obese and suffer all sorts of health problems when they grow older.'

'Aunt Tabatha, really . . . ' Eva tried in vain to interject.

'Since, however, you have put them out in honour of my visit,' the old woman continued, 'I will have a couple myself, and the children may also have one each, so as not to spoil their appetites.' The formidable lady gave Eva an uncharacteristic wink before handing the dish round to the children.

All three of the Petunias, seated side by side on the sofa, their hair parted and suits neatly pressed, declined politely.

'No, thank you,' they chorused in angelic unison, after which Aunt Tabatha commended them on their restraint.

'It's marvellous,' she said. 'What amazing children.'

The afternoon passed without a hitch, although Aunt Tabatha regretfully had to decline the tea that Eva had prepared, having eaten far too many biscuits. Eventually she departed, sweeping theatrically from the room, but not before pausing once again to praise Eva for her wonderful parenting skills and to give each of the bewildered children an approving pat on the head. As soon as the front door closed, the children jumped up from the sofa, and rushed to their mother in a state of considerable agitation.

'Mummy, why did Auntie Tabatha eat Fido's biscuits?' asked Jamie, nine, and the eldest of Eva's progeny.

'Ew, it's disgusting,' cried seven-year-old Barney, thinking that maybe his aunt was, in fact, a dog herself.

'I always knew she was mad,' said Eva's youngest, Rosie, tearfully, for she was wondering what poor Fido was going to have for his tea.

She needn't have worried. That night the Petunias' dog, Fido, feasted on a platter of smoked-salmon sandwiches, followed by scones and raspberry jam served with fresh cream, and the children looked forward with frenzied excitement to Aunt Tabatha's next visit, wondering with glee what the crazy old woman would eat this time.

TIME'S WINGED CHARIOT

'But at my back I always hear
Time's winged Chariot hurrying near;
And yonder all before us lie
Deserts of vast Eternity.'
– ANDREW MARVELL, '*TO HIS COY MISTRESS*'

'Most of us spend our lives as if we had another one in the bank.'
– BEN IRWIN

'As I get older the years just fly by. I don't think there was an April this year.' – JEREMY HARDY, COMEDIAN

'Half our life is spent trying to find something to do with the time we have rushed through life trying to save.' – WILL ROGERS, COMEDIAN AND ENTERTAINER

'One day, aged forty-five, I just went into the kitchen to make myself a cup of tea, and when I came out I found I was sixty-eight.'
– THORA HIRD, ACTRESS

'No matter how much time you save, at the end of your life, there's no extra time saved up. You'll be going, "What do you mean there's no time? I had a microwave oven, Velcro sneakers, a clip-on tie. Where's the time?" But there isn't any. Because when you waste time in life they subtract it. Like if you saw all the Rocky movies, they deduct that.' – JERRY SEINFELD, ACTOR AND COMEDIAN

'Don't save things "for best". Drink that vintage bottle of wine – from your best crystal glasses. Wear your best designer jacket to go down to the post office to collect your pension. And, every morning, spritz yourself with the perfume you save for parties.' – GERALDINE MAYER

'Guinness is a great day-shortener. If you get out of bed first thing and drink a glass, then the day doesn't begin until about 12.30 when you come to again, which is nice. I try to live in a perpetual snooze.' – QUENTIN CRISP, WRITER AND ACTOR

'Years grow shorter but days grow longer. When you're over seventy, a day is an awful lot of time.' – CARL SANDBURG, POET AND WRITER

'I wasted time, and now doth time waste me.'
– WILLIAM SHAKESPEARE, *RICHARD II*

'There is never enough time unless you're serving it.'
– MALCOLM FORBES, PUBLISHER OF *FORBES MAGAZINE*

FOOD FOR THOUGHT

There are a number of ways in which senior moments can be, if not fully eradicated, then at least greatly reduced. A healthy, well-balanced diet is of course essential, but there are certain foodstuffs which, when eaten regularly, are particularly beneficial in helping to boost the mental faculties and fight against a whole range of diseases. Central to keeping our wits intact and staving off senior moments is looking after that most crucial of organs: the brain.

An intake of vital nutrients is essential for a healthy brain. Without a doubt the body's most complex organ, the brain not only controls our motor functions, such as breathing and walking, but it also holds sway over our speech, our sensory perceptions, our emotions and our memory. Here is a guide to get you started on the kind of healthy eating plan or diet that will keep your wits sharpened and your mind focused. All you have to do now is remember where you put that shopping list . . .

Eggs

Eggs are not only one of the best 'fast foods' available, they are also a wonderful source of protein, as well as being packed full of all the essential amino acids required to build the brain's neurotransmitters. For instance, eggs contain tryptophan, which is required to make serotonin – the antidepressant mood-enhancer that is the basis for many pharmaceutical products. Whenever possible it is best to purchase organic, free-range eggs as these will not only have been laid by happier hens, but they will also contain lower cholesterol levels than those laid by battery hens.

Fish

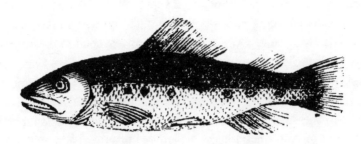

The benefits of eating fish are second to none. Scientific research has conclusively shown that fish, particularly those high in omega-3 fatty acids, such as salmon, mackerel, sardines and tuna, can help keep the brain healthy. Research has shown that people between the ages of sixty-five and ninety-four who eat fish at least once a week are at a significantly lower risk of developing Alzheimer's disease than those who eat no fish at all. Other benefits of this deep-sea equivalent to pure gold include a significant reduction in the risk of suffering a stroke, and aiding memory processes. One only has to look to Japan, where the diet includes vast amounts of fish, to see the advantages of a fish-filled diet: on average, a Japanese person is likely to outlive his or her British counterpart by at least ten years.

Lean Meat

Because the brain needs a constant supply of amino acids in order to produce neurotransmitters (the brain's messengers), protein (particularly in meat, which contains all eight essential amino acids) is a key ingredient of any well-balanced diet. However, the fat which often accompanies meat is of no nutritional value whatsoever. As a result, it is important to buy lean meat such as skinless chicken. Indeed, chicken (particularly free-range chicken) is an ideal source of protein since it contains far less saturated fat than many red meats such as lamb and beef.

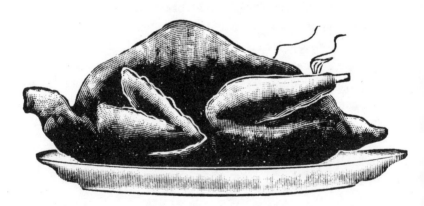

Olive Oil

Many readers may be familiar with a household game called 'hunt the olive oil'. This usually occurs just when you're about to fry onions and normally entails opening every cupboard in the kitchen in the vain hope that one of them might contain the aforementioned oil. When you do finally find the bottle, for some reason known only to the olive-oil fairy, it is usually lurking in the fridge, or occasionally hiding in the wine rack. Of course, once you have located it, the hunt is then on for the onion, which you have probably put down during your quest for the oil. I hear you ask, gentle reader, is all this palaver really worth it? Well, the answer is yes, because olive oil is fundamentally made up from a combination of monounsaturated fatty acids and antioxidant substances. In particular, extra virgin olive oil, which comprises the first pressing of the olives, has been shown to offer protection from heart disease and help maintain low cholesterol levels.

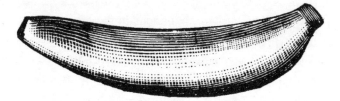

Bananas

The joy of bananas is that no matter what state your teeth are in, you can always manage to consume one just by sucking! Not only this, but the high levels of potassium contained in bananas makes them an excellent fruit for preventing strokes, improving energy levels and lowering our blood pressure, as well as reducing the risk of contracting diabetes.

Strawberries

We all know the problem of parking the car in a multi-storey and then not being able to find it again; well, the same difficulty appears to apply in a field of 'pick your own' strawberries when you put down your punnet in search of fatter, juicier fruit and then spend the next half hour searching for the damned container. If blueberries are small, dark purple flavour-bombs, then strawberries are the red equivalent (and about half the cost). Rich in fibre, they offer a good amount of vitamin C, as well as containing beta carotene (an important antioxidant), folic acid and potassium – all of which help regulate blood pressure. In addition to this, strawberries are one of the very few fruits rich in ellagic acid, which can help in the fight against carcinogens, as well as being packed full of antioxidants.

Blueberries

Blueberries have been shown to work physiological wonders – boosting the memory and replenishing the brain's grey cells; improving eyesight; protecting against Alzheimer's, heart disease and various forms of cancer; while also lowering cholesterol levels. Despite (or perhaps because of) this, supermarkets have frequently sold out of them; if by some miracle there is a good stock of blueberries on the shelves, then the likelihood is that you could book yourself a Caribbean cruise for the price of a mere punnet. Complaints aside, blueberries have been shown to contain a higher concentration of antioxidants than any other fruit, so try adding a handful to your breakfast cereal or porridge each morning to reap the benefits.

Beetroot

If you are prone to the shakes, beetroot is probably not the best vegetable to consume, as trying to remove the stains from your clothing could quickly become a full-time occupation. On the other hand, because it is high in anthocyanidins, which protect the brain's most delicate cell membranes and make them more receptive to neurotransmitter messages, beetroot is an excellent source of brain food. In addition to this, beetroot also contains high levels of iron which help the blood to carry oxygen to the brain and keep it in tip-top working order. Fresh and cooked beetroot are best, as these contain the most nutrients, whilst pickled beetroot normally contains less vitamins and minerals.

Broccoli

This dark green vegetable is packed full of nutrients, all of which are vital to normal brain function. Loaded with vitamin C (three ounces of cooked broccoli contain more vitamin C than two oranges), as well as minerals such as iron, calcium and potassium, broccoli is one of those foods that protects the brain from oxidative damage. Always aim to choose the darkest green heads, for these contain the highest nutrient levels, and make sure you store them in a cool dark place until you are ready to cook them, then steam or boil for two to three minutes to preserve every last ounce of goodness.

Red Peppers

Red peppers are simply green peppers that have been allowed to ripen for longer, thus ensuring they contain a greater level of nutrients. Indeed, red peppers are a wonderful source of vitamin C and other antioxidant substances. When choosing peppers try to avoid any that are shrivelled or dull in appearance as these will probably have lost a lot of their vitamin C content. Bright, firm peppers are best.

Carrots

Eyesight not too good? Keep bumping into the furniture? Can't thread a needle or locate your children? Then get a new pair of glasses. On the other hand, if you're in need of vitamin A, the nutrient essential for fighting off free radicals within the body, your best bet is to eat lots of carrots. The bright orange colour of this root vegetable is the best indicator that it is packed full of beta carotene, a substance which converts to vitamin A when it is ingested. Carrots contain more beta carotene than any other vegetable, although sweet potatoes run a close second; both are packed full of brain-protecting antioxidants. Try to choose the darkest orange examples, for these will contain the highest levels of beta carotene, and always steer clear of old-looking, shrivelled specimens, as their vitamin content will be greatly depleted.

Avocados

A common misconception concerning both old people and avocados is that they contain a very high fat content and therefore should be avoided at all costs. This is wrong at least as far as avocados are concerned, for although they certainly contain fat, most of it is of the monounsaturated variety which does not clog up the arteries or cause heart disease. Avocados are also rich in the antioxidant vitamins A, C and E, as well as the mineral potassium, which helps protect against mental confusion and depression.

Tomatoes

So long as you don't get the pips stuck in your dentures, tomatoes are little red bombs of goodness. Packed full of lycopene, which acts as a powerful antioxidant, tomatoes can help protect both the brain and the nervous system. In addition to this, tomatoes are also a wonderful source of a wide range of minerals and B vitamins, which fuel the brain and create a steady supply of neurotransmitters. Always try to choose the freshest tomatoes available and eat them as soon after purchase as possible. Though not packed with quite as much goodness as their kissing cousins, the tinned variety provides an easy alternative to fresh tomatoes.

Molasses

As long as you don't open a tin of molasses, stick your spoon in and then rush through the house to answer the phone, molasses are a marvellous food, albeit a nightmare to clean off the floor. Sourced from sugar cane, this rich, dark brown, sticky substance is packed full of brain-boosting nutrients such as manganese, iron, copper, calcium and magnesium, as well as all the B vitamins required to build neurotransmitters. Two tablespoons of molasses contain more calcium than an average size glass of milk and more iron than a medium or large egg. Try adding a little molasses to your porridge oats in the morning or to any other dish that requires sweetening. Alternatively, put a couple of teaspoons of blackstrap molasses in a mug and add boiling water for a comforting hot drink.

Nuts

'God gives nuts to those with no teeth.' – ARABIC PROVERB

As well as frequently feeling and acting nuts, it can also be extremely useful for those battling senior momentitis actually to eat nuts. As nuts containing both omega-3 and omega-6 fatty acids, both of which are essential for keeping our brains in tip-top working order, a regular intake of nuts, either eaten as a snack or added to other foods such as our morning cereal, is highly recommended. Several recent scientific studies have further shown that the omega-6 fatty acid found in nuts may help to slow down the progression of Alzheimer's disease.

Wholegrains

As we grow older our bowel movements can often become a problem. Fear not, however, because if you consume a sensible amount of wholegrains, the problem can normally be resolved in a couple of days. Moreover, wholegrains can help in the fight against two of the world's leading killers: heart disease and cancer.

The definition of a wholegrain is that all three parts of the grain are kept intact, including the fibre-rich outer layer and the nutrient-filled germ. Wholegrains also contain vitamins, in particular B vitamins and vitamin E, as well as minerals such as magnesium and iron and complex carbohydrates.

Studies have shown that including three portions of wholegrains in your daily diet can reduce cholesterol levels, as well as the risk of suffering from diabetes, heart disease, strokes and a number of cancers. Try eating wholegrain brown bread instead of highly refined white bread; brown rice instead of white rice; and wholewheat pasta instead of normal pasta.

Water

It is one of life's funny little laws that as we grow older, so our bladders grow weaker, but don't let this put you off drinking copious amounts of water, as this is undoubtedly one of the biggest health boosts you can give your body. The brain is composed of nearly 93 per cent water, while our blood is composed of approximately 82 per cent; it therefore goes without saying that water is an important part of our chemical make-up.

Drinking between one and two litres of water a day will help our bodies flush out toxins, whilst also improving our concentration and maintaining the skin's elasticity. Other health benefits include reducing the risk of colon and bladder cancer, as well as helping with everyday complaints such as constipation. Bottled water is probably best, but an alternative is to process tap water through a filter. Water is surely the easiest, most cost-efficient way of keeping your body in good condition.

Remember that although drinks such as tea and coffee are made up with water, an excess of these beverages can lead to dehydration.

THANKS FOR THE MEMORIES

On his way home from work a young man sees an old lady sitting on a park bench, crying her eyes out. Stopping in concern, he asks her what is wrong.

'I have a fit young husband who makes love to me every morning and then gets up and makes me pancakes with blueberries, sausages, bacon, fried eggs, mushrooms, fresh fruit and freshly ground coffee.'

'Well, why on earth are you crying, then?'

'Every day he makes me a delicious lunch of lamb chops and new potatoes, followed by chocolate cake, then we watch a film together and make love for the rest of the day.'

'Well, then why are you crying?'

'For dinner he makes me a gourmet meal with a bottle of red wine, and then we make love until two in the morning.'   .

Beginning to lose patience, the young man asks again, 'Why are you crying?' Shaking uncontrollably, the old woman sobs,

'I can't remember where I live!'

FIGHTING FIT

Sleep Well

'Oh, Sleep! it is a gentle thing
Beloved from pole to pole!'
– SAMUEL TAYLOR COLERIDGE, '*THE RIME OF THE ANCIENT MARINER*'

There can be no more pleasurable way to keep senior moments at bay and to maintain a youthful appearance than indulging in plenty of sleep. Indeed, it is essential that we enjoy plenty of sleep throughout our lives, but never is it more valuable than during our senior years.

If you find dropping off to sleep difficult, then perhaps you should revert to those tried-and-tested methods of a hot bath and a milky drink before bed. Reading will also help to relax the mind and prepare it for sleep. Other tips include:

- keeping your bedroom well aired

- drinking camomile tea before you go to bed

- counting sheep

Reduce Alcohol

Apart from the obvious effects that alcohol consumption has on our brains, drinking too much beer, wine or spirits can also interfere with the absorption of all the key nutrients, particularly two stress-busting vitamins, vitamin B1 and B2, that are needed to help maintain a healthy mind and body.

Alcohol consumption also contributes to radical changes in our blood sugar levels, which can result in depression and anxiety. Try to keep your alcohol consumption to a minimum, particularly in hot weather when dehydration is a very real risk.

Avoid Junk Food

Just because you either a) forgot to buy anything for dinner, or b) successfully located the shopping list, found the supermarket and returned with your shopping bags, only to burn your meal, there is no excuse for buying and consuming junk food and then pretending that it's good for you.

Junk food contains unnaturally high levels of sugar, thus causing enormous fluctuations in our blood sugar levels, leading to loss of concentration and increased irritability. The high levels of sugar also tend to cause short bursts of energy followed by long periods of lethargy, while the high fat content of most junk food can cause clogging of the arteries and reduce the flow of blood to the brain.

Reduce Caffeine Intake

Contrary to popular belief, rather than boosting your energy levels, a cup of coffee in the morning can have precisely the opposite effect, significantly increasing your blood pressure and raising your stress levels. Drinking cup after cup of coffee is an extremely bad idea, particularly if you want to maintain an even concentration throughout the working day and enjoy unbroken sleep throughout the night.

If you think your caffeine consumption is exacerbating stress, don't suddenly stop drinking it, as this can cause headaches, but try to wean yourself off it over a period of weeks. Try substituting decaffeinated coffee for your morning fix, whilst also introducing yourself to herbal and fruit teas, as well as other hot drinks which have a zero caffeine content.

Don't Smoke

There can be no one on earth who is unaware of the many hazards of smoking, a habit that can lead to any number of diseases and, at worst, cost you your life. But, even if you avoid smoking-related diseases such as lung cancer and emphysema, the habit could be wreaking more subtle, but nonetheless harmful effects upon your body. Smoking speeds up the ageing process so that, for example, a forty-year-old smoker will almost certainly be 'biologically' older than a forty-year-old non-smoker. Smoking also affects our skin's appearance as it produces oxygen-free radicals which accelerate the formation of wrinkles and other skin disorders, while also increasing the risk of developing non-melanoma skin cancers.

Bearing all the above information in mind, the best gift any smoker could give themselves would be to kick the habit as soon as possible. These days there are numerous aids to help the smoker stop, including nicotine patches and nicotine chewing gum, as well as alternative therapies such as hypnosis. Visit your doctor and talk through all the options, before deciding on which course of action is best for you. Make sure you reward yourself, too; giving yourself little treats along the way to encourage you to keep going is a great incentive. Finally, if you don't succeed at first, try not to become despondent, or feel you have failed. Simply take a step back, reassess your choice of method, and start again.

'I gave up smoking, without the aid of pills, hypnotism or patches, seventeen days ago, having been told that if I didn't I mightn't have a leg to stand on. Well-meaning friends hastened to assure me that within forty-eight hours I would see an improvement in my complexion, my eyes, my hair. Needless to say, I'm still looking.

What I have noticed, and deplore, is a return of my sense of smell. I had no idea that the odour of leftover food could pervade a house. Nor had I realized that I would regrow hairs in my nose, causing prolonged fits of sneezing.' – BERYL BAINBRIDGE, 'FAGS FOR THE MEMORY', *THE OLDIE*

Stay Out Of The Sun

Nothing is more guaranteed to bring on a senior moment than looking at yourself in the mirror and realizing that your once-perfect, blemish-free skin is now more wrinkly than an elephant's bottom. Even tiny amounts of ultraviolet radiation can trigger the process which leads to wrinkly skin. In fact, the role the sun plays in prematurely ageing skin cannot be stated strongly enough. Exposure to ultraviolet radiation (commonly referred to as UVA or UVB) which emanates from sunlight accounts for almost 90 per cent of symptoms associated with premature skin ageing. To prevent this from happening it is advisable never to sit in direct sunlight for more than half an hour per day, and even this is dangerous unless you are protected by a sun lotion with a high (25–30) UVA/UVB factor.

NATURAL REMEDY

Memory loss is probably the primary cause of senior moments – neglecting to remember that we have told that story before, failing to recall what we have spent the last half an hour looking for, not having the foggiest idea where we left our glasses, even committing the heinous crime of forgetting the names of our own children. But do not despair; there are natural remedies that can help sharpen the memory as well as improve our overall health and wellbeing.

Take, for example, gingko biloba. The oldest living tree species, the ginkgo is thought to have been growing on earth for 150 – 200 million years and is one of the most thoroughly researched herbs in the world. It is rapidly gaining recognition as a memory enhancer because of its beneficial effects on the vascular system and the cerebellum. It is also thought that ginkgo can aid circulation, counteract the effects of ageing and fatigue, as well as help to relieve tension and anxiety.

Ginkgo works by increasing blood flow to the brain, helping to improve short and long term memory, increasing mental clarity and speeding up reaction time. It is also often used to treat Alzheimer's, as well as complaints such as fatigue, confusion, depression or a lack of concentration and energy. The herb has further been used in treatment of circulation disorders and studies have shown that ginkgo increases blood flow to the retina. The many and varied benefits of this remedy, as well as the fact that it is entirely natural, mean that it is a great way to beat senior moments and improve overall health and wellbeing.

MNEMONICS

Mnemonics is the term used for a system of aiding the memory by employing any number of devices such as stories, abbreviations, rhymes, diagrams and acronyms, among others, to help store and recall new information. Such techniques are an invaluable resource for those of us in the grip of senior momentitis, who feel that our brains, once capable of holding so much, are now beginning to resemble sieves, incapable of retaining any manner of useful information such as names, dates, faces, birthdays and appointments for longer than thirty seconds.

The ancient Greeks, who understood that memory was an important tool that required training, were the first to use the system of mnemonics, but there are many modern instances of the practice. Common examples include the 'Thirty days hath September' rhyme for remembering the number of days in each month, and 'Every good boy deserves favour' to recall musical notation. Although these examples are taken from the classroom, many such devices can be employed by the older generation who might feel that their memory could be sharpened or improved.

Repetition and association are the two key components of any memory technique. Repetition involves familiarizing yourself with a list; memorizing it; replicating it; and then checking over it until you are sure you know it. Association is somewhat more complicated. Studies have shown that knowledge is more efficiently stored in the long term when it is associated with anything that is familiar. It follows that by associating new information with familiar stories, images and words, you can effectively store it for longer. Association is a technique that calls for imagination and creativity, connecting everyday facts with fictional worlds; by the time you have fully explored and perfected this technique, your associations will be original and unforgettable.

Here are some basic techniques to get you started:

Sentences:
If you are trying to memorize a list in order, try making a sentence using the initial letters of the words you are aiming to remember.

Visualizations:
Create a striking mental image that incorporates the information you need to memorize.

Abbreviations:
Use the first letter of each word, even though it doesn't spell out a word. This is a short and concise way of turning complex and longer information into bite-size, manageable pieces.

Acronyms:
If you are trying to memorize a list that is fairly short and the order of the words is not significant, try making a word using the first letter from each word that needs to be remembered.

Loci System:
Create visual associations with locations with which you are already familiar. An example of this might be compiling a shopping list in which each item corresponds to a room in your house.

Link Method:

One of the easiest mnemonic techniques is the link method, which works by making connections between items in a list, linking them either with a flowing image or with a story which features them. The progression of the story and the visual impact of the images give you the glue to recall effectively otherwise disparate items. Take the first image and, creating a connection between this and the next item, move through the list linking each item with the next.

Story Method:

Although it is possible to remember lists of words using association only, it is more helpful to fit the associations into a story; otherwise by forgetting just one association you can lose the whole of the rest of the list. The story method, in which images are linked together as part of a story, makes it easier to remember the order of events and it can also help to improve your ability to remember information if you forget the sequence of images. It can be a lot of fun as well, so get your thinking caps on!

LAST-MINUTE OBSERVATIONS
PLUS A FEW EXTRA TIPS

'Always go to other people's funerals, otherwise they won't come to yours.' –YOGI BERRA, BASEBALL PLAYER AND MANAGER

'When grace is joined with wrinkles, it is adorable. There is an unspeakable dawn in happy old age.' – VICTOR HUGO, WRITER

'I have never killed a man, but I have read many obituaries with great pleasure.' – CLARENCE DARROW, LAWYER

'To hold the same views at forty as we held at twenty is to have been stupefied for a score of years, and take rank, not as a prophet, but as an unteachable brat, well birched and none the wiser.' – ROBERT LOUIS STEVENSON, WRITER

'You know you are getting old when the candles cost more than the cake.' – BOB HOPE, ENTERTAINER

'Do not regret growing older. It is a privilege denied to many.' – ANON

'A man's only as old as the woman he feels.' – GROUCHO MARX, ENTERTAINER

'And in the end, it's not the years in your life that count. It's the life in your years.' – ABRAHAM LINCOLN, FORMER PRESIDENT

'Young men think old men are fools, but old men know young men are fools.' – GEORGE CHAPMAN, PLAYWRIGHT AND POET

'Those whom the gods love grow young.' – OSCAR WILDE, WRITER

'I used to hate going to weddings – all those old dears poking me in the stomach and saying, "You're next." But they stopped all that when I started doing the same to them at funerals.' – GAIL FLYNN

'Don't worry about avoiding temptation – as you grow older, it starts avoiding you.' – MICHAEL FORD, AUTOMOBILE MANUFACTURER

'Dying is a very dull, dreary affair. And my advice to you is to have nothing whatever to do with it.' – W. SOMERSET MAUGHAM, PLAYWRIGHT AND WRITER

'Old age is an excellent time for outrage. My goal is to say or do at least one outrageous thing every week.' – MAGGIE KUHN, ACTIVIST

'We need old friends to help us grow old and new friends to help us stay young.' – LETTY COTTIN POGREBIN, EARLY LEADER IN WOMEN'S MOVEMENT

'It is so comic to hear oneself called old, even at ninety I suppose.' – ALICE JAMES, WRITER

'I'm dying, but otherwise I'm in very good health.' – EDITH SITWELL, POET AND CRITIC

'It takes a long time to become young.' – PABLO PICASSO, ARTIST

'If I had any decency, I'd be dead. Most of my friends are.' – DOROTHY PARKER, WRITER AND POET

'When you are younger you get blamed for crimes you never committed and when you're older you begin to get credit for virtues you never possessed. It evens itself out.' – I.F. STONE, INVESTIGATIVE JOURNALIST

'Death is nature's way of saying your table is ready.' – ROBIN WILLIAMS, ACTOR AND COMEDIAN

'Life is a great surprise. I do not see why death should not be an even greater one.' – VLADIMIR NABOKOV, WRITER

'I don't have a warm personal enemy left. They've all died off. I miss them terribly because they helped to define me.' – CLARE BOOTHE LUCE, EDITOR AND PLAYWRIGHT

'Anyone who stops learning is old, whether at twenty or eighty. Anyone who keeps learning stays young. The greatest thing in life is to keep your mind young.' – HENRY FORD, AUTOMOBILE MANUFACTURER

'Dying is no big deal. The least of us will manage that. Living is the trick. My life has been strawberries in the wintertime, and you can't ask for more than that.' – RED SMITH

'If I'm ever stuck on a respirator or a life-support system, I definitely want to be unplugged. But not until I'm down to a size 8.'
– HENRIETTE MANTEL, ACTRESS

'We learn from experience that man never learns from experience.'
– GEORGE BERNARD SHAW, PLAYWRIGHT

'Memorial services are the cocktail parties of the geriatric set.'
– JOHN GIELGUD, ACTOR

'One consolation of ageing is realizing that while you have been growing old your friends haven't been standing still in the matter either.' – CLARE BOOTHE LUCE, EDITOR AND PLAYWRIGHT

'Experience is a comb life gives you after you lose your hair.'
– JUDITH STERN

'Inside every seventy-year-old is a thirty-five-year-old asking, "What happened?"' – ANN LANDERS, ADVICE COLUMNIST

'I expect you know the story of Winston [Churchill] in later years in the House of Commons. When a colleague tactfully told him that several of his fly buttons were undone, he said, "No matter. The dead bird does not leave the nest."' – RUPERT HART-DAVIS, *THE LYTTELTON – HART-DAVIS LETTERS*

'I don't mind dying. Trouble is, you feel so bloody stiff the next day.' – GEORGE AXELROD, WRITER AND PRODUCER

'I am ready to meet my Maker. Whether my Maker is ready for the ordeal of meeting me is another matter.' – WINSTON CHURCHILL, FORMER PRIME MINISTER

'I have learned throughout my life as a composer chiefly through my mistakes and pursuits of false assumptions, not by my exposure to wisdom and founts of knowledge.' – IVOR STRAVINSKY, CLASSICAL COMPOSER

'Jesus died too soon. If he had lived to my age he would have repudiated his doctrine.' – FRIEDRICH NIETZSCHE, PHILOSOPHER

'I shall not die of cold. I shall die of having lived.'
– WILLA CATHER, WRITER

'The answer to old age is to keep one's mind busy and to go on with one's life as if it were interminable. I always admired Chekhov for building a new house when he was dying of tuberculosis.'
– LEON EDEL, LITERARY CRITIC

'I'm not afraid of death. It's the stake one puts up in order to play the game of life.' – JEAN GIRAUDOUX, DRAMATIST

'I believe you should live each day as if it was your last, which is why I don't have any clean laundry, because who wants to wash clothes on the last day of their life?' – JACK HANDEY, COMEDIAN

'It was Death – possibly the only dinner guest more unwelcome than Sidney Poitier.' – KINKY FRIEDMAN, SINGER AND SONGWRITER

BIBLIOGRAPHY

Burningham, John. (Ed.)
The Time of Your Life – Getting On With Getting On
(Bloomsbury, 2002)

Chancellor, Alexander.
'Senior Disservice'
(*The Guardian*, 15 May 1999)

Clark, Alan.
Alan Clark: Diaries
(Weidenfeld & Nicholson, 1993)

Corcoran, Alan, and Green, Joey.
Senior Moments
(Simon & Schuster, 2002)

Coward, Noel.
The Noel Coward Diaries
Edited by Graham Payn and Sheridan Morley
(Weidenfeld & Nicolson, 1982)

Enright, D. J.
Play Resumed – A Journal
(Oxford University Press, 1999)

Jarski, Rosemarie.
Wrinklies' Wit & Wisdom
(Prion, Carlton Publishing Group, 2005)

Mortimer, John.
The Summer of a Dormouse
(Viking, 2000)

Priestley, J. B.
Outcries and Asides
(Heinemann, 1974)

Zobel, Allia.
The Joy of Being 50-Plus
(Workman Publishing, 1999)